Metalcraft
Theory and Practice

John R Bedford M Coll H

City and Guilds Final Certificates, Woodwork and Metalwork
Formerly Head of Technical Subjects, Steyning Grammar School, Sussex
Author of *A Basic Course of Practical Metalwork, Metalwork Projects,*
  and *Graphic Engineering Geometry*

New International Metric Standards Edition

John Murray   Fifty Albemarle Street   London

PREFACE

This book is the product of considerable experience of teaching metalwork both in industry and in schools. It has been prepared to meet the needs of students for the 'O' level G.C.E. examinations in Metalwork, Craftwork and in Engineering Workshop Theory and Practice. It also covers the requirements of the Certificate of Secondary Education as well as sections of the General Course in Engineering (Workshop Practice) and the course for Mechanical Engineering Technicians.

The coverage is extensive for so modest a volume as the visual method of treatment presents maximum information in condensed form. No attempt has been made to exhaust the subject nor catalogue the whole range of metalworking tools. The aim has been rather to display the essential and more commonly used tools and processes in a manner which facilitates rapid learning and easy revision. This visual presentation of the subject should prove particularly suitable to the ever-increasing number of home-workshop enthusiasts, developing their understanding of technology. It is sincerely hoped that this volume with its new approach will play its part in the training of those interested in metalwork, be they students, junior engineers or amateur enthusiasts, to develop skills and understanding worthy of the great traditions of the craft.

PREFACE TO THE METRIC EDITION

This new metric edition has been prepared following extensive consultations with manufacturers of engineering tools, machines and materials. It complies with the appropriate new Metric Standards of the British Standards Institution and the International Standards Organisation. Because the next few years will be a transitional period, details of obsolete but still widely used metalworking units are retained in parenthesis alongside the metric ones which replace them.

Acknowledgements

The examination questions at the end of the book are reproduced by kind permission of the Examining Boards listed below, to whom the author expresses his grateful acknowledgements.

Associated Examining Board (*AEB*)
Cambridge University Local Examinations Syndicate (*CLE*)
Joint Matriculation Board (*JMB*)
University of London (*UL*)
Oxford Delegacy of Local Examinations (*OLE*)
Southern Universities Joint Board (*SUJB*)
Welsh Joint Education Committee (*WJEC*)

Associated Lancashire Schools Examining Board (*ALSEB*)
East Anglian Examinations Board (*EAEB*)
Metropolitan Regional Examinations Board (*MREB*)
Middlesex Regional Examinations Board (*MEB*)
South-East Regional Examinations Board (*SEREB*)
Southern Regional Examinations Board (*SREB*)
West Midlands Examination Board (*WMEB*)

© John R. Bedford 1967, 1971
First published 1967
Second edition (New International Metric Standards Edition) 1971
Reprinted 1972, 1975, 1976, 1977, 1978, 1980, 1982, 1985, 1988, 1990, 1993

Printed in Great Britain at The Bath Press, Avon

ISBN 0 7195 2251 X

CONTENTS

PRODUCTION OF IRON

Iron is the most commonly used metal in everyday manufacture. This is owing to its low cost and widespread availability, its great strength, the readiness with which it may be cast into intricate shapes and its alloying properties. It occurs naturally in combination with other elements as ores, some of which, such as magnetite, and the red and brown hematites, are richer in iron than others. The iron is separated from the ore by smelting with coke and limestone in a blast furnace.

The ironmaking process is a continuous one, running day and night for about five years, by which time the furnace lining begins to crumble and needs to be replaced. Iron ore, together with coke for a fuel and limestone as a flux, is continuously tipped into the furnace through double bell lids which open one at a time to prevent the furnace gases escaping into the atmosphere. These gases are led off from the top of the furnace through a dust catcher into a stove where they are mixed with air and burnt, thus heating a series of chequered brick tiles inside the stove to a high temperature. The valves A and B in the diagram below are open with C and D closed. At the appropriate moment the burning gases are switched to a second stove. Valves A and B are closed and C and D are opened. Air is then pumped through the hot stove, thus becoming pre-heated to about 550 °C. It is then blown through the bustle pipe and the tuyeres into the heart of the blast furnace. This hot blast causes the coke to burn fiercely providing the necessary heat. At the same time carbon monoxide from the burning coke rises up through the charge where it combines with the iron oxides, reducing them to iron. This spongy mass settles down the furnace, heating up on the way until it reaches the hearth in fluid form. At the same time, the limestone combines with the impurities to form a liquid slag which floats on top of the molten iron.

When sufficient metal has been produced, usually about every four hours, the slag is first run off through the slag notch. The clay stopper in the tapping hole is next removed allowing the molten metal to run out. In some foundries this is cast into 'pigs'. These are blocks of convenient size, sometimes run into moulds in the sand floor but more often into steel moulds in a pig-casting machine. In other foundries it is run into huge crucibles for transport to a nearby steel furnace.

A great proportion of the annual production of iron is converted directly into steel. About a quarter of the total is made into castings (car cylinder blocks, machine tool frames, etc.) with a very small amount being worked into wrought iron for forging (chain making).

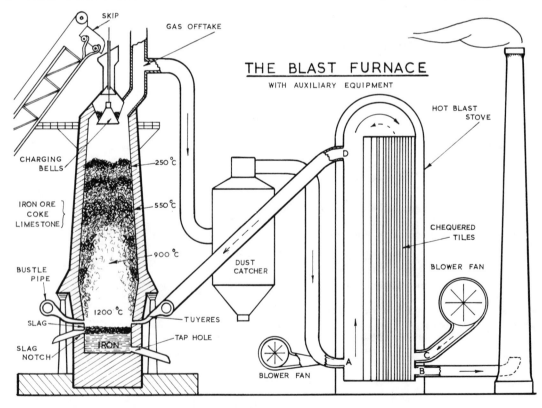

THE BLAST FURNACE
WITH AUXILIARY EQUIPMENT

CEMENTATION FURNACE

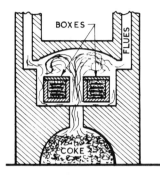

CRUCIBLE FURNACE

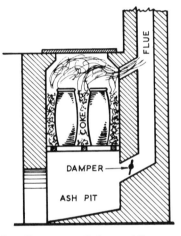

CONVERSION OF IRON TO STEEL

Steel is produced by refining the iron to rid it of the many impurities absorbed during smelting, and then combining carbon in varying proportions as desired up to a maximum of 1.7%.

The *cementation* process was the first method regularly employed to produce steel. It consisted of packing iron bars surrounded with charcoal into airtight fireclay boxes. These sealed containers were then heated to 1100 °C for about three weeks during which time the hot bars absorbed carbon from the charcoal. This carbon content was largely in the skin of the metal where it imparted a characteristically blistered appearance, hence the name 'blister' steel.

In order to provide a more uniform dispersal of the carbon the steel rods were bundled together, reheated and hammered out to their original size again. The resultant metal was termed 'shear' steel and whilst of better quality than blister steel the process proved slow and costly.

The *crucible* method, discovered by Benjamin Huntsman in Sheffield in 1740, made possible a more reliable production of high-grade tool steel. In this process, blister steel bars from the cementation furnace were packed together with charcoal into crucibles which were then sealed and placed in a box furnace and surrounded with coke which burned at intense heat. At the appropriate moment the crucibles were lifted from the furnace, skimmed and poured into an ingot mould.

This method is still used in small-scale production of high-class tool steels, but it was superseded for the mass production of steel by the Siemens open hearth furnace which in its turn is now being displaced by the modern oxygen injection process.

The discovery of the *puddling* process by Henry Cort in 1784 led to the first great expansion in the iron and steel industry. In this process molten iron was poured into a shallow bath in a reverberatory furnace. This was a furnace where direct contact between fuel and metal was avoided, the flame being driven across the roof of the furnace above the surface of the molten metal. Iron ore was added to oxidise the impurities. Meanwhile the charge was continually stirred with a long iron 'raddle' or bar to expose the metal to the heat and the chemical action of the oxide. As the impurities oxidised, the iron stuck to the raddle in a large rounded ball or 'bloom'. The puddler then removed this bloom from the furnace and passed it to the mill. Here the hot bloom was hammered and rolled to squeeze out the combined slag. Some of this slag remained dispersed in fine threads throughout the bars of 'wrought iron' imparting a characteristic fibrous structure to the metal.

This metal was worked into plates and bars, the most important single item being railway lines. About half the production from the mid-nineteenth-century blast furnaces went to the puddling furnaces until the development of the Bessemer converter produced steel which was plentiful and both cheaper and stronger than wrought iron.

PUDDLING FURNACE

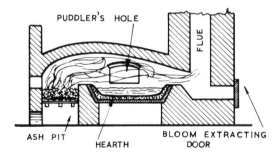

In the mid-nineteenth century steelmaking was a slow and costly business quite unable to keep pace with demand. Henry Bessemer, seeking a new process, noted that the essential part of the puddling process lay in the 'burning' away of excess carbon, partly by exposing it to oxygen in the air and also by chemical reaction with the oxygen in the iron oxide. This gave him the idea of blowing air through the molten iron in order to convert it to steel. In 1856 he first demonstrated his 'converter'. This process revolutionised steelmaking by producing a better quality metal cheaply and at a fast rate.

Converters are pear-shaped crucibles built of firebricks within a casing of mild steel plates. The acid converter is lined with silicious bricks whilst the basic converter is lined with dolomite (magnesian limestone) bricks.

In operation, the converter is tipped to the horizontal and molten iron is poured in. The air blast is turned up and the converter is returned to the vertical position, the air meanwhile being blown through the metal in fine streams. In the 'acid' process, silicon present in the iron oxidises to a slag and produces heat during the reaction. This slag absorbs oxides of iron and manganese which are also present in the iron. The carbon then oxidises and 'burns' away. Any sulphur and phosphorus which was present in the original iron is carried over into the steel. In the 'basic' process, (developed by Thomas and Gilchrist in 1879) a quantity of lime is first tipped into the converter followed by the liquid iron. The silicon, manganese and iron oxide melt to form a slag and this is joined by the lime. When the end of this part of the process is reached there is an 'afterblow' of a few minutes during which the phosphorus is removed. The molten steel is skimmed clear of slag and poured off into ladles from which it is usually teemed into ingot moulds. The ingots from these moulds are re-heated and passed to the reduction mills for suitable shaping.

Modern improvements in steelmaking have come from the use of oxygen gas instead of air to 'burn' out the impurities in the molten iron. A lance is lowered into the crucible and through this oxygen is blown at high speed directly on to the surface of the molten metal. This effects a very rapid conversion and produces a good quality steel.

The most widely used process is the Austrian 'LD-OLP' (Linz-Donauwitz, Oxygen-Lance-Powder). In this, a flux of powdered lime is injected into the oxygen blast to assist in slag formation

THE BESSEMER CONVERTER
BLOWING POSITION

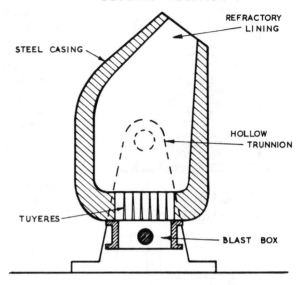

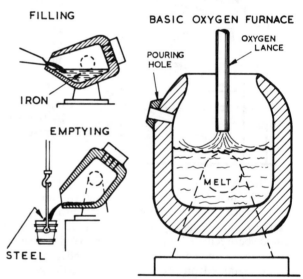

and so clean the steel. In the 'Kaldo' process (developed in Sweden by Dr Kaling at Domnarvet) the converter is rotated whilst the oxygen is being injected. Another rotating method (developed in Germany) is the 'rotor' process. This has two separate oxygen lances, one injecting directly into the molten metal whilst the other one blows oxygen across its surface. Known collectively as the 'basic oxygen process' this has virtually replaced Bessemer Converters and is rapidly becoming the major method of steelmaking today. The Basic Oxygen Furnace takes about 30% scrap with 70% molten iron and converts this to steel at a rate of 350 tonnes in 40 minutes.

SIEMENS' OPEN HEARTH FURNACE

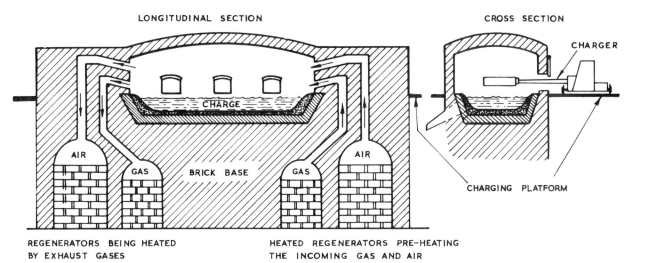

LONGITUDINAL SECTION

CROSS SECTION

CHARGER

AIR

GAS

CHARGE

BRICK BASE

GAS

AIR

CHARGING PLATFORM

REGENERATORS BEING HEATED
BY EXHAUST GASES

HEATED REGENERATORS PRE-HEATING
THE INCOMING GAS AND AIR

This method of steelmaking was developed by the Siemens brothers in England in the mid-nineteenth century. Incorporation of the regenerative system of furnace heating rendered the process so efficient that it has since produced about three-quarters of the world's supply of steel.

In this furnace the metal is contained in a shallow bath which is surrounded by walls and a roof of firebricks. In the front wall are sliding doors through which the raw materials are inserted by a mobile crane. The charge is made up of molten iron from the blast furnace, together with scrap and pig iron. In the back wall is the tap hole. In the side walls are openings, or ports, through which pre-heated gas (usually from the blast furnace) and air are blown into the furnace. These mix and burn with a very hot flame above the bath of molten metal, raising it to a temperature of about 1650 °C. The hot exhaust gases leave through ports in the opposite wall, passing through and heating chambers of chequered brickwork. A similar set of chambers is situated at the opposite side of the furnace and valves are fitted which permit the direction of flow of both gas and air to be reversed so that heat exhausted from the furnace is used to pre-heat the incoming gases. A modern development is the use of oil as fuel. This is sprayed into the furnace under pressure where it burns with a higher temperature than blast furnace gas, thus producing a quicker melt.

There are two types of furnace: 'Acid' and 'Basic'. The one used to produce 'acid' steel has a lining of silica bricks. The slag floating on top of the molten metal oxidises the impurities silicon, carbon and manganese, but does not remove the sulphur and the phosphorus. Hence only iron having a very low content of the latter impurities can be used in an acid furnace.

'Basic' steel is produced in a furnace lined with dolomite (magnesian limestone) and lime is worked into the molten slag. This removes all the impurities including both sulphur and phosphorus.

The whole process takes about 10 hours to convert 350 tonnes of iron to steel. On completion, the steel is run off through the furnace tapping hole into huge ladles and poured from these into ingot moulds. As soon as these ingots have solidified they are transferred to gas-heated soaking pits where they are kept ready for the rolling mills.

The latest development in open hearth steelmaking, which is claimed to double output, is the 'Ajax' process. In this, oxygen is blown through lances at a very high speed directly on to the surface of the molten metal. This intensifies the rate of chemical reaction and thus increases the speed of production. This however, cannot compete with the new basic oxygen process, and Open Hearth Furnaces are now being superseded by the more economical Basic Oxygen Furnace detailed at the foot of page 6.

ELECTRIC FURNACES

A small amount of steel is produced from electrically heated furnaces. These are of two distinct types: the Electric Arc Furnace and the High Frequency Induction Furnace.

The Electric Arc Furnace is heated by arcs struck between graphite electrodes suspended through the furnace roof and the metal charge in the hearth. This furnace usually has a 'basic' lining (see page 6) and the molten metal is fully refined. Each melt takes about two hours and refines from 10 to 30 tonnes of metal.

The High Frequency Induction Furnace is heated by the resistance of the charge to an induced current flowing within itself. This develops from a very high frequency current carried in a large coil which surrounds the furnace casing. The Induction Furnace is mainly used for straight melting operations where the scrap metal used in the charge is selected to give the required characteristics to the finished melt, and little if any refining is done. The charge varies from 500 kg to 5 tonnes.

No fuel is burnt inside either of the furnaces, therefore the slag, the furnace atmosphere, the temperature of the melt and the resultant steel can be controlled to precise requirements. Thus these furnaces are used for the production of small amounts of high grade special alloy steels.

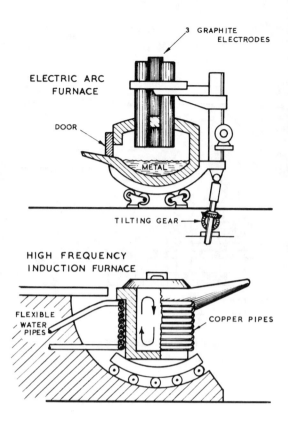

ALLOY STEELS

Steels are often classified in three grades according to their carbon content.

Mild steel, up to 0.25% carbon
Medium Carbon steel, from 0.25% to 0.7% carbon
High Carbon steel, from 0.7% to 1.5% carbon

In addition to these, there is a large group termed 'Alloy Steels' which contain significant amounts of elements other than iron and carbon. A few are listed below.

Type	Main components	Characteristics and uses
Manganese steel	Iron with 3 to 14% manganese	Highly resistant to wear. Non-magnetic. Stone crushers, dredger buckets.
Molybdenum steels	Iron with up to 0.7% molybdenum	Tough but malleable. Excavator shovels, spades.
Nickel steels	Iron with 6 to 30% nickel	Nickel refines grain structure and increases strength. Corrosion resistant. Turbine blades, car engine valves.
Invar	Iron with 36% nickel	Extremely low expansion rate when heated. Pendulums, survey tapes.
Nickel-chrome steels	Iron with 1 to 5% nickel and up to 2% chromium	Corrosion resistant, air hardening. Heavily loaded machinery, armour plate.
Stainless steels	Iron with 4 to 15% chromium	Corrosion resistant. Cutlery and cooking utensils.
Tungsten steels	Iron with 10 to 18% tungsten	Resistant to frictional heat. Cutting tools, wire drawing dies.

A fourth group of steels, from which most modern cutting tools are made, is termed 'High Speed Steels'. Their chief characteristic is their ability to retain edge hardness when working at high speeds. A typical composition is: Iron with 0.75% carbon, 0.3% each silicon and manganese, 15% tungsten, 4% chromium, 3% vanadium.

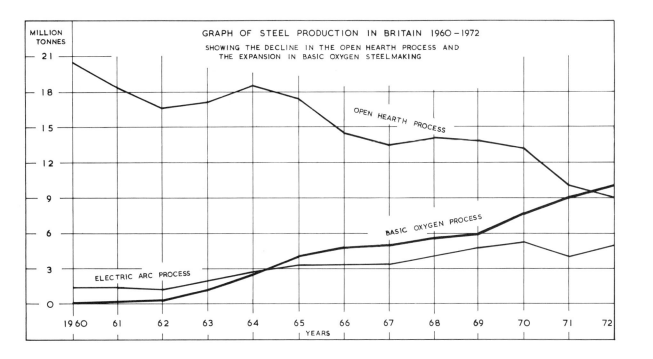

GRAPH OF STEEL PRODUCTION IN BRITAIN 1960 – 1972
SHOWING THE DECLINE IN THE OPEN HEARTH PROCESS AND
THE EXPANSION IN BASIC OXYGEN STEELMAKING

FLOW CHART OF FERROUS METAL PRODUCTS

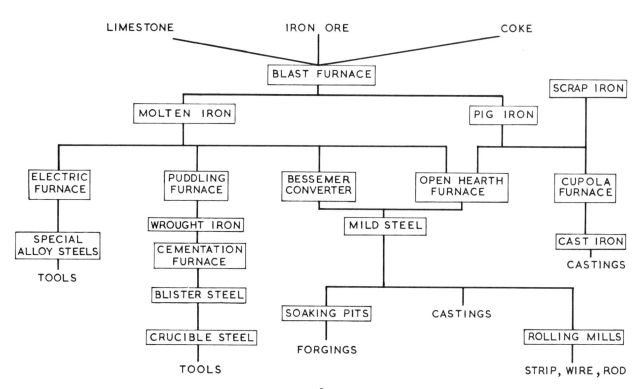

ALUMINIUM

Aluminium ore is more abundant throughout the earth's crust than that of any other metal. All clays consist largely of aluminium silicate but no satisfactory method has been developed whereby this and other aluminium compounds may be reduced to the metal in an economic manner. The only commercial source of aluminium is the ore bauxite (impure alumina or aluminium oxide), so named because it was first discovered in the district of Les Baux in southern France.

Tiny globules of the pure metal were first produced by chemical means in 1825 by Hans Oersted, a Danish chemist, and again by Wöhler, a German chemist in 1827. Various chemical methods of obtaining the metal were employed for the next 60 years but as these were both tedious and expensive there was little metal produced. Indeed, it was actually listed as a precious metal and sold by the ounce in the early nineteenth century. The first commercial process for the manufacture of the metal was established in 1856 based on the method developed by Henri Deville, a French chemist. Production was still slow and costly and comparatively little metal was made, however, until in 1886 Paul Herault in France and Charles Martin Hall in America simultaneously discovered the method of reduction by electrolysis.

Production methods were further improved in 1894 by Karl Bayer's developments in the processing of alumina from bauxite. The Bayer process consists of mixing the crushed roasted ore with a hot caustic soda solution. This dissolves the aluminium hydroxide as sodium aluminate leaving all the impurities in suspension. These are removed by filtration and the aluminate solution is then pumped into tall precipitation tanks. As this cools down a small quantity of pure aluminium hydroxide crystals is added. This is known as the 'seed charge'. This seeding sets off a precipitation of crystals from the solution. These crystals are washed to remove all traces of caustic soda and then roasted in rotating tubular kilns. This produces fine white crystals of pure alumina.

The alumina is then reduced to the metallic state by the Hall-Herault process. In this the alumina is stirred into a bath of molten cryolite (a fluoride of aluminium and sodium) contained in a reduction cell.

This is a mild steel box 5m x 3m x 1m lined with a layer of carbon which serves as the cathode. The anodes are thick carbon rods suspended from busbars. An electric current of some 30 000 amperes at 6 volts flows between the anodes and the cathode. The heat from this maintains the cryolite in a molten state at 1000 °C. The molten cryolite dissolves the alumina and the passage of the electric current then decomposes it into aluminium and oxygen. The oxygen combines with the carbon of the anode forming carbon dioxide which passes out of the top of the cell whilst the metal sinks to the bottom and is periodically drawn off and cast into ingots. The process is a continuous one, alumina being constantly worked into the surface crust and molten aluminium drawn off at the bottom. The cryolite remains virtually unaffected by the process; the carbon rods slowly burn away and are periodically replaced. The natural cryolite ore is found only in Greenland but it can now be synthesised. As it requires about 18 000 kilowatt-hours of electricity to produce one tonne of aluminium it is economically essential to site reduction plants close to sources of cheap electricity. This is usually in mountainous regions where hydro-electric power is plentiful and cheap.

As cast from the cell the metal is over 99% pure and a large proportion of it is used in this state. As this pure metal has little strength, small quantities of other metals are alloyed with it to improve its qualities. The first discoveries in aluminium alloying were made by Dr Wilm when he found that the addition of small quantities of magnesium produced an alloy which after full heat-treatment proved to be five times as strong as the pure aluminium. This led to the development of the 'duralumin' alloy, which in its turn inspired further research, thus producing the many specialised aluminium alloys in use today.

ALUMINIUM FURNACE

OR REDUCTION CELL

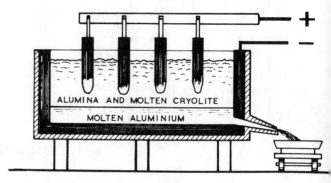

ALUMINA AND MOLTEN CRYOLITE

MOLTEN ALUMINIUM

TIN

Tin has been smelted and used by man throughout recorded history. Its ore, cassiterite, is frequently found with malachite, one of the copper ores, and it was probably a smelting of an accidental mixture of these two ores which produced the very first alloy. This new metal proved harder than either of its parent metals and gave its name to that stage in man's history known as the 'bronze age'.

Cassiterite is found in veins of rock in Cornwall and in Bolivia, where it is mined by traditional methods. In the rest of the world the ore occurs as pea-sized gravel in alluvial beds from which it is recovered by three different methods:

1 Where the beds are under water the ore is dredged by an endless chain of buckets from a floating dredger.

When in an open-cast mine it is either

2 washed out of the working face by high pressure water jets, or

3 dug out by mechanical excavators.

The ore is crushed to powder, washed and dried and then roasted in a reverberatory furnace to rid it of sulphur and to oxidise other impurities. After this refining process the ore is again washed, mixed with slaked lime and anthracite and again smelted, when after a thorough fluxing it is run off into ingot moulds.

Almost half of the world's output of tin is used by the tinplate industry; about one fifth in the manufacture of solders; and the remainder for alloying. The principle alloys are: bearing metals, bronze, gun metal and bell metal.

TINPLATE

There are two methods of producing tinplate; the original 'hot dip' process in which sheets of mild steel are passed through a layer of zinc chloride flux floating on a bath of molten tin, and the modern process of tinning by electrolysis. This latter is by far the most common, accounting for about 80% of the world's output of tinplate. The process begins with the welding together of large coils of hot rolled mild steel to form one long continuous strip. This is then passed through a long tank containing a 10% acid solution which dissolves the surface oxide scale produced by hot rolling. After pickling, the clean strip is washed in hot water and then dried in hot air. It is then given its coating of tin by being passed through a deep rubber-lined tank which is filled with a suitable tin–salt solution. Anodes of pure tin are suspended in the bath and current is fed through rollers to the moving steel strip, thus making it the cathode. The thickness of the coating can be varied but is usually maintained at about 0.001 mm. After it has left the electrolyte the coated strip is momentarily heated to melt the surface of the tin and then immediately cooled. This produces the characteristic bright silvery appearance. Finally, the strip is given a thin coating of oil and sheared into standard-sized sheets.

COPPER

Copper has been found in the metallic state in a number of places and because of this was probably the first metal used by man. There are a number of copper ores; malachite, containing about 55% copper, and copper pyrites, containing about 35% copper, are the most commonly used ones.

To extract the metal the ore is first crushed and sieved. It is then roasted to remove the sulphur. The calcined ore is then smelted in a reverberatory furnace to produce a 'matte' of metal containing about 70% crude copper, the remainder being oxides and other impurities. The matte is poured into a converter and air is blown through the molten metal to oxidise the impurities in a manner similar to the Bessemer process in steelmaking.

The refined metal is then cast into slabs which are termed 'blister' copper because of the blistered appearance of the metal. Blister copper is then further refined either by a second roasting in a reverberatory furnace to remove the combined oxygen, or by an electrolytic process using anodes of blister copper, a cathode of refined pure copper and concentrated copper sulphate for an electrolyte. The flow of electric current through the cell builds up pure copper on the anode, the impurities falling to the bottom as sludge. The product from this latter process is known as 'electrolytic' copper.

There is a greater tonnage of copper produced than that of any other non-ferrous metal. About half of this is used for electrical requirements.

LEAD

Although lead is one of the heaviest of metals it is also one of the softest, so it is used where easy working is required but where strength is not important. It is highly resistant to corrosion and has been in use for water supply and drainage systems for well over a thousand years. The Romans made great use of it for these purposes, obtaining most of their supplies from British mines.

Galena is the principal lead ore. It is a compound of between 83% and 86% lead, the remainder being sulphur and other impurities, including silver. The extraction of silver is often a by-product of the lead smelting process. The lead ore is first passed through a crushing mill and then through a 'flotation' washer which separates out the impurities according to their different gravities. The 'dressed' ore is then placed in a blast furnace where the oxide is reduced by carbon from the coke, the heat being sufficient to melt both the metal and the slag.

In addition to its uses in the pure state, lead is widely used for alloying. White metal bearings used in high speed machinery contain 40% to 80% lead with copper, tin and antimony. Printers' type metal contains about 80% lead, 18% antimony and 2% tin.

ZINC

Pure zinc boils and turns to a vapour at bright red heat, so it cannot be smelted by the conventional process of heating in a fierce fire. This is probably why the metal was not isolated for centuries after the discovery of brass, European zinc being first produced on a commercial basis by William Champion in Bristol in 1740.

The commonest zinc ore is zinc blende, which is a compound of zinc and sulphur. In the first stage of manufacture the ore is crushed and washed in a 'flotation' process which clears it of impurities. The concentrated zinc sulphide is then roasted in a reverberatory furnace where zinc oxide is formed and the sulphur driven off as sulphur dioxide. This is collected and converted to sulphuric acid.

In the second stage the metal can be obtained from the zinc oxide either by smelting and distillation or by electrolysis. Each process is responsible for about half of the world's production of zinc.

In the smelting process the zinc oxide is mixed with a suitable carbon such as powdered coal or anthracite, pressed into small briquettes and then heated to about 1100 °C in a special furnace. The

zinc vaporises at this temperature and is led off through a pipe at the top of the furnace and into a closed container where it is cooled and so condensed into liquid zinc.

In the electrolytic process the zinc oxide is dissolved in dilute sulphuric acid. This is purified and used as an electrolyte in a cell fitted with lead alloy anodes and aluminium cathodes. As the heavy current flows through the cell, zinc is deposited on the cathodes from which it is stripped off every 24 hours. The zinc is then melted and cast into ingots.

A modern and still expanding development in the use of zinc lies in the production of pressure die castings. This was made possible by the careful re-distillation of zinc to produce a metal of 99.99% purity. This is then alloyed with 4% aluminium, 1% copper and 0.05% magnesium. Because of its cheapness, low melting point and good casting characteristics this alloy is the most widely used die casting metal today.

Galvanizing

Zinc is highly resistant to corrosion in the air and so is much used for protective purposes. Iron and steel articles are frequently given a coating of zinc for this reason and when so treated are said to be 'galvanized'. The zinc coating can be deposited on the steel either by electrolysis or by dipping the articles in a bath of molten zinc. The galvanizing industry uses about half the world's production of zinc. Zinc can be sprayed on to items such as ships' hulls and pylons which are too large for the normal galvanizing process. In the process, known as 'sherardising', small items are 'tumbled' with powdered zinc in a revolving drum at a temperature of 370 °C for a few hours, by which time the zinc has diffused into the skin of the steel parts.

Alloys

An alloy is a metallic mixture composed of two or more elements, one of which is a metal. A notable feature of modern industry is the immense number of different alloys in everyday use. Many of these have wide applications, whilst others are confined in scope having been developed for highly specialised purposes.

Some alloys produce properties intermediate between the parent metals. Others exhibit characteristics quite different from those of the component metals. Often the melting point of the alloy is significantly lower than those of the original metals and the hardness and strength are markedly altered.

COPPER BASE ALLOYS

	Brasses—copper plus zinc			
Parts per cent			Name	Uses
Copper	Zinc	Others		
90	10	—	Gilding metal	Jewellery and art metalwork
70	30	—	Cartridge brass	Deep drawing. Very ductile
66	34	—	Standard brass	For presswork
62	37	1 tin	Naval brass	Resistant to sea-water corrosion
60	37	3 lead	Free cutting brass	Easy to machine at high speeds. Does not bend
60	40	—	Muntz metal	Hot water fittings
	Bronzes—copper plus tin			
90	—	10 tin	Gun metal	Load carrying bearings
78	—	22 tin	Bell metal	Sonorous and resonant. For bell founding
	Other copper base alloys			
63	27	10 nickel	Nickel silver	Tableware, costume jewellery
92	—	{ 0.5 phosphorus 7.5 tin	Phosphor bronze	Engine bearings, ships propellers
97	2.5	0.5 tin	Coinage bronze	Coinage

TIN, LEAD AND WHITE METAL ALLOYS

Parts per cent			Name	Uses
Tin	Lead	Others		
60	40	—	Fine solder	Quick-setting soft solder for electrical work
50	49	1 antimony	Tinman's solder	General purpose soft solder
30	69	1 antimony	Plumber's solder	Plumbers' wiped joints (extended pasty stage)
80	20	—	Pewter	Art metalwork costume jewellery
90	—	10 antimony	Britannia metal	Cheap jewellery, art metalwork
90	—	7 antimony 3 copper	Babbitt metal	White metal bearings for high speed spindles
3	82	15 antimony	Type metal	Printers' type (expands slightly on cooling thus giving sharp outlines)
14	24	12 cadmium 50 bismuth	Wood's metal	Fusible plugs, low temperature casting. Melting point, 65 °C

ALUMINIUM ALLOYS

There are some 40 standard aluminium alloys of which about half are used for casting and half for wrought work. The commonest casting alloy is LM 4. This is composed of 92% aluminium, 5% silicon and 3% copper. Another common casting alloy is LM 6, composed of 88% aluminium with 12% silicon. This latter alloy is very free flowing when cast. Duralumin is the oldest aluminium alloy still in use and is used for pressings and sheet metal work but not for casting. It is made up of 4% copper, 0.5% each of silicon, manganese and magnesium, with the remainder aluminium. This alloy has the property of slowly hardening over a period of about five days, which is known as 'age hardening'.

ZINC ALLOYS

There are two standard zinc casting alloys in common use: one with 3% copper, 4% aluminium, 0.1% magnesium and the remainder zinc; the other with 0.1% copper, 4% aluminium, 0.05% magnesium and the remainder zinc. The first mentioned alloy has greater strength than the latter though it is not as stable, losing some of this strength through ageing. Zinc alloys are susceptible to inter-crystalline corrosion and for this reason must be made up from zinc which is at least 99.99% pure. Both alloys cast well taking a good finish and requiring only low casting temperatures.

FERROUS METALS

Material	Appearance	Relative density	Melting point °C	Approximate proportions of constituents	Handling characteristics	Uses
Cast iron	Grey with a granular surface. Rough castings show the joint line of the mould.	7200 (S.G. 7.2)	1200 —1400	93% iron, 3% carbon with traces of sulphur, silicon, manganese, and phosphorus.	Brittle, has a softer core beneath a hard skin. Strong in compression but snaps before it will bend. Cannot be forged. *Dropping*—gives out a dull note. *Drilling*—produces small chips that crumble easily *Grinding*—gives a few dull sparks, some bursting. *Filing*—produces small grey chips with a fine black powder. *Quenched from red heat*—no change. (May crack.)	Main castings for machine frames and beds especially for sliding ways as the free carbon forms a lubricant. Car piston rings. Castings for domestic hot water boilers.
Wrought iron	Scaly, usually covered with a fine red rust.	7850 (S.G. 7.8)	1600 —1700	99% iron plus 1% of impurities including carbon, sulphur, silicon, manganese and phosphorus.	Soft, malleable and ductile. Bends well hot or cold. Forges and welds well. *Dropping*—gives a dull note with a metallic ring. *Drilling*—white curly shavings with slag cracks. *Grinding*—fair quantity of bright sparks. *Filing*—file drags and produces white grains with black slag. *Quenched from red heat*—no change.	Crane hooks and chains. Anchor chains. Cores for electric motors and transformers.
Mild steel	Bright drawn mild steel has a smooth white surface. Black mild steel is covered with blue grey oxide.	7800 (S.G. 7.8)	1300 —1500	Up to 0.25% carbon. The remainder is iron plus traces of impurities including sulphur, silicon, manganese and phosphorus.	Tough and ductile. Bends readily but fractures with repeated bending. Forges well. *Dropping*—gives out a ringing note. *Drilling*—produces long grey curled shavings. *Grinding*—shower of long white sparks. *Filing*—solid and resistant with an even texture. *Quenched from red heat*—little change, slightly toughened.	Bridges, girders, wires, tubes, bolts, nuts, general workshop uses.
Cast steel (Carbon steel, Tool steel)	Smooth skin of black oxide.	7900 (S.G. 7.9)	1200 —1400	0.5 to 1.5% carbon. The remainder is iron plus traces of impurities, including sulphur, silicon, manganese and phosphorus.	Tough, fairly ductile when annealed yet is brittle when hardened. Forges well but is resistant under the hammer. *Dropping*—gives out a high ringing note. *Grinding*—moderate number of full red sparks. Difficult to drill, saw or file being tough and dense in structure. *Quenched from red heat*—becomes hard and brittle.	Springs and most tools, such as drills, taps, dies, punches, chisels, sets, shear blades, hammer heads.

NON-FERROUS METALS

Material	Appearance	Density	Melting point °C	Approximate proportions of constituents	Handling characteristics	Uses
Aluminium and its alloys	Light grey, showing a bright silver-white when machined.	2560 (S.G. 2.6)	658	100% aluminium is an element.	Light in weight. Malleable and ductile. Takes a good polish and is resistant to corrosion. Machines easily giving off long white curly shavings. Difficult to solder and weld owing to the rapid forming of oxide.	Foil wrappings for sweets and foodstuffs. Cooking utensils. Car body panels. Its light weight makes it particularly useful in the aircraft industry where the alloys are used for engine castings and sheets for cladding the air-frames.
Copper and its alloys	Brownish pink	8820 (S.G. 8.8)	1083	100% copper is an element.	Extremely ductile and malleable either hot or cold when in the annealed state. Good conductor of heat and electricity. Solders easily.	Soldering bits, tubing, rivets, electrical wiring. Some roofing work.
Brass	Yellow	8400 (S.G. 8.4)	930 1010	Alloys of varying quantities of copper and zinc.	The varying proportions of copper and zinc affects the physical properties of the alloys. Cannot be worked at red heat as it crumbles at this temperature. Solders easily. Takes a good polish.	Castings, rivets, water fittings, wire, screws, stampings.
English standard brass	Yellow			66% copper, 34% zinc	English standard brass. Ductile and malleable.	
Turning quality brass	Yellow			60% copper, 37% zinc, 3% lead	Turning quality brass giving off small chips when machined.	Rods for turned work such as screws, valves, spindles.
Gilding metal	Golden colour	8600 (S.G. 8.6)		90% copper, 10% zinc	Malleable and ductile. Solders easily. Takes on a good polish.	Costume jewellery, vases, trays.
Bronze	Dark yellow	8800 (S.G. 8.8)		88% copper, 10% tin, 2% zinc	Highly resistant to corrosion. Machines well producing small chips. Tough.	Castings and bearings, especially for marine work.
Tin	Bright silvery white	7290 (S.G. 7.3)	231	100% tin is an element.	Extremely ductile and malleable. Does not oxidise appreciably. Not used much on its own.	Protective coating on steel plate (tinplate). Used with other metals to form alloys.
Zinc	Blueish white	7100 (S.G. 7.1)	419	100% zinc is an element.	The sheet metal folds easily and can be soldered. Castings are brittle and show clearly visible grains. Resistant to atmospheric corrosion.	Protective coating on mild steel (galvanising). Sheets are used for roofing. Castings are used in many industries. Zinc is often used with other metals to form alloys.
Lead	Blue-grey. The cut metal shows a dull metallic lustre.	11 370 (S.G. 11.4)	327	100% lead is an element.	Extremely plastic and malleable. Can be soldered but is usually fused. Highly resistant to atmospheric corrosion.	Water pipes, sheets for roofing and gutters. Accumulator plates in car batteries.

ANNEALING Softening and relieving internal stresses. Involves heating to a required temperature and cooling slowly. Mild steels are heated slightly above the upper critical point; high carbon steels are heated just above the lower critical point; copper and brass to a dull red heat; aluminium is rubbed with soap and heated until the soap turns black—this indicates the correct heat for annealing aluminium.

BRITTLENESS Breaks comparatively easily when subjected to a sharp blow.

CARBURISING (case-hardening) Mild steel is heated to bright red and thickly coated with a carbon compound. The steel absorbs carbon, thus producing a high carbon steel skin over a soft steel core. See page 56.

CONDUCTIVITY The ability to conduct heat or electricity.

DUCTILITY Bends, twists and stretches without fracture.

ELASTICITY The ability to return to its original shape after a deforming force is removed.

FERROUS METALS Metals containing iron. (Non-ferrous metals do not contain iron.)

FLUX A substance which combines with oxides and removes them from molten metals thus facilitating fusion.

HARDENING Produces maximum hardness by heating to a suitable temperature and quenching. See page 56.

HARDNESS The ability to resist cutting or abrasion by other tools.

LUBRICATION The elimination of friction between metal surfaces by interposing a thin film of oil between the two.

MALLEABILITY Withstands hammering and rolling without cracking.

NITRIDING A form of case-hardening where a casing of iron-nitride is produced by holding steel in ammonia vapour.

NORMALISING Refining the grain structure, thereby producing a more evenly textured metal with normal tensile strength.

REFRACTORIES Materials which are able to withstand high temperatures without melting or crumbling, e.g. firebricks and crucibles.

TEMPERING Relieving the hardening stresses and reducing the hardness of the metal. See page 57.

TENSILE STRENGTH A measure of the load, usually a straight pull, at which a material will fracture or cease to be stretched.

MEASURING AND MARKING OUT

Accurate marking out is the first step in all processes and the methods and instruments are common to all metalworking crafts. Measurements are taken either from one edge made straight or from a centre line. Scriber lines on non-ferrous metals and oxide covered steels are readily visible but bright steel needs coating with copper sulphate solution or 'engineer's blue' (Prussian blue oil paint) if the line is to be easily seen.

Measuring and testing are continuous processes throughout manufacture whether working with hand tools or machines. Degrees of accuracy are specified on the workshop drawings. Measuring methods in order of accuracy are:

Direct measurement from a rule
Calipers set to a rule
Calipers set to a plug gauge
Vernier calipers
Micrometer readings
Dial indicator gauge

WHEN MARKING OUT AND TAKING MEASUREMENTS THE RULE SHOULD BE TILTED TO BRING THE GRADUATIONS INTO CONTACT WITH THE WORK

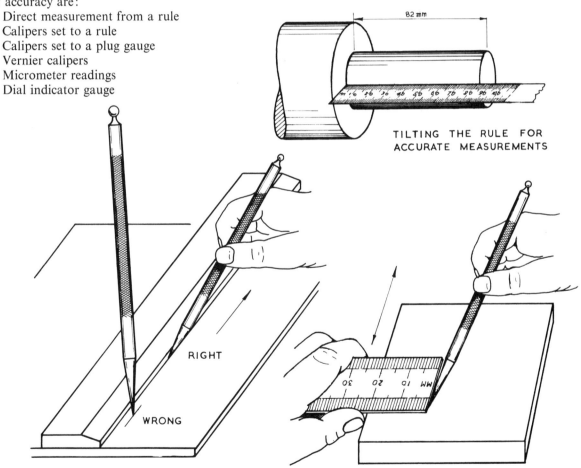

WORK

TILTING THE RULE FOR ACCURATE MEASUREMENTS

RIGHT

WRONG

ERROR IN MARKING OUT CAUSED BY FAILING TO RUN THE SCRIBER POINT AGAINST THE STRAIGHT EDGE

A QUICK METHOD OF MEASURING IN FROM AN EDGE

CENTRING ROUND BAR

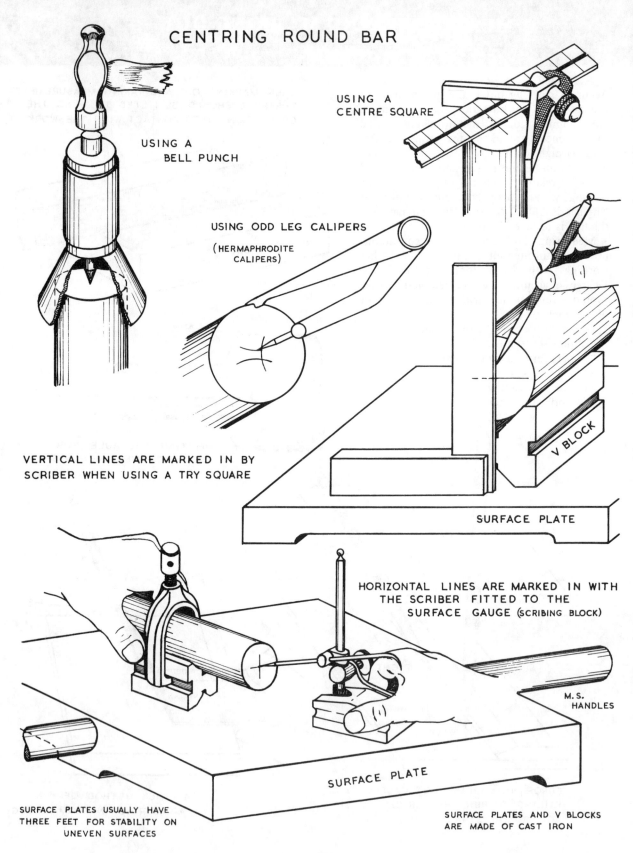

USING A
CENTRE SQUARE

USING A
BELL PUNCH

USING ODD LEG CALIPERS

(HERMAPHRODITE
CALIPERS)

V BLOCK

VERTICAL LINES ARE MARKED IN BY
SCRIBER WHEN USING A TRY SQUARE

SURFACE PLATE

HORIZONTAL LINES ARE MARKED IN WITH
THE SCRIBER FITTED TO THE
SURFACE GAUGE (SCRIBING BLOCK)

M. S.
HANDLES

SURFACE PLATE

SURFACE PLATES USUALLY HAVE
THREE FEET FOR STABILITY ON
UNEVEN SURFACES

SURFACE PLATES AND V BLOCKS
ARE MADE OF CAST IRON

PARALLELS

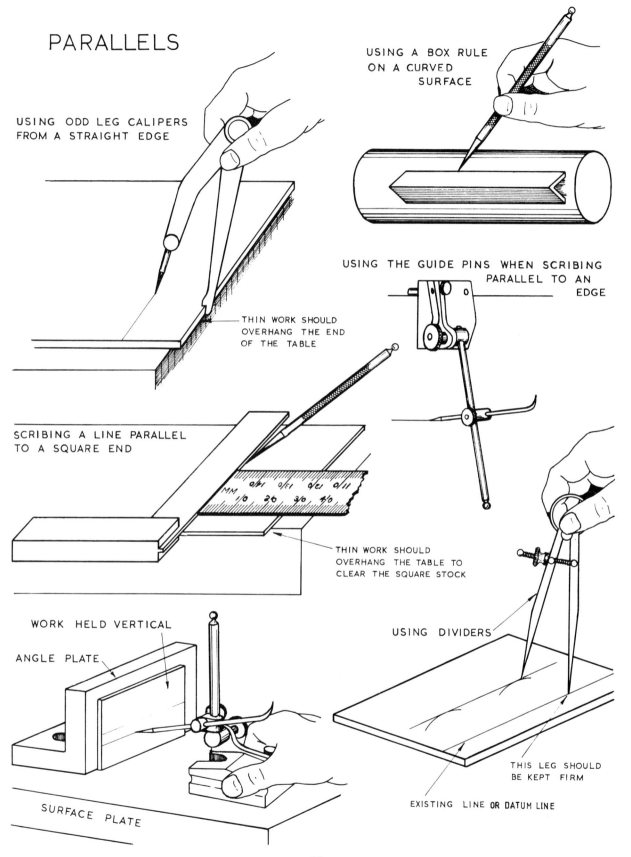

USING ODD LEG CALIPERS
FROM A STRAIGHT EDGE

USING A BOX RULE
ON A CURVED
SURFACE

THIN WORK SHOULD
OVERHANG THE END
OF THE TABLE

USING THE GUIDE PINS WHEN SCRIBING
PARALLEL TO AN
EDGE

SCRIBING A LINE PARALLEL
TO A SQUARE END

THIN WORK SHOULD
OVERHANG THE TABLE TO
CLEAR THE SQUARE STOCK

WORK HELD VERTICAL

ANGLE PLATE

USING DIVIDERS

THIS LEG SHOULD
BE KEPT FIRM

SURFACE PLATE

EXISTING LINE OR DATUM LINE

CALIPERS

BOW SPRING   FIRM JOINT

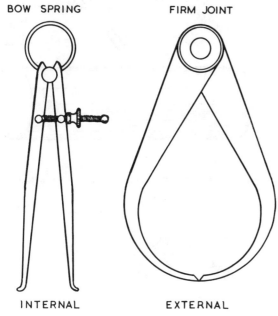

INTERNAL   EXTERNAL

MAKING FINE ADJUSTMENTS

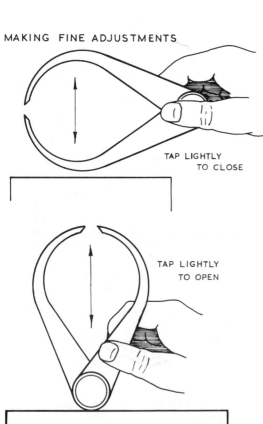

TAP LIGHTLY
TO CLOSE

TAP LIGHTLY
TO OPEN

MEASURING WITH EXTERNAL CALIPERS

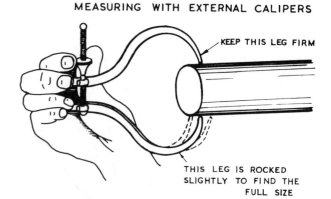

KEEP THIS LEG FIRM

THIS LEG IS ROCKED
SLIGHTLY TO FIND THE
FULL SIZE

SETTING THE CALIPERS
OR READING OFF A MEASUREMENT

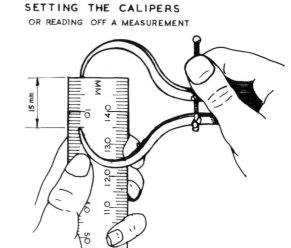

15 mm

MEASURING WITH INTERNAL CALIPERS

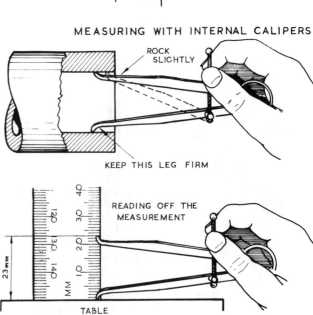

ROCK
SLIGHTLY

KEEP THIS LEG FIRM

READING OFF THE
MEASUREMENT

23 mm

TABLE

MICROMETER CALIPER

EXTERNAL O-25mm

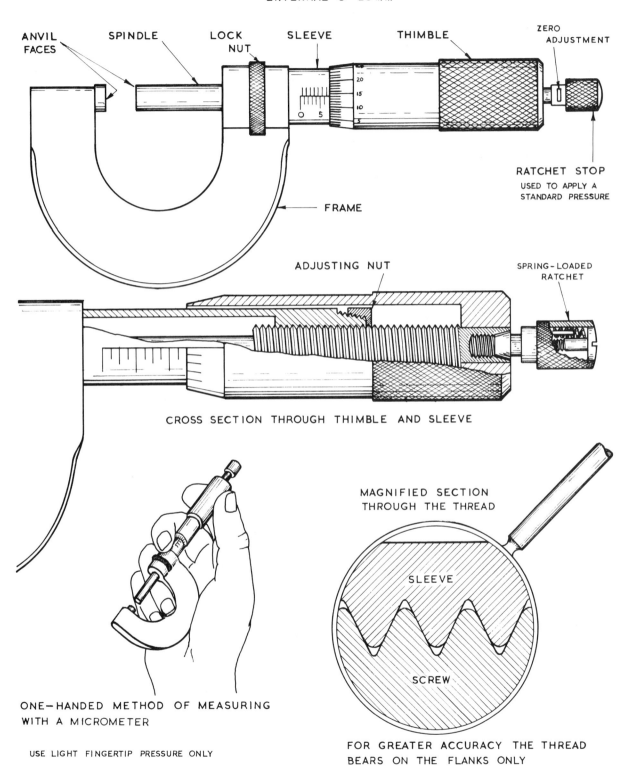

ANVIL FACES

SPINDLE

LOCK NUT

SLEEVE

THIMBLE

ZERO ADJUSTMENT

RATCHET STOP
USED TO APPLY A
STANDARD PRESSURE

FRAME

ADJUSTING NUT

SPRING-LOADED RATCHET

CROSS SECTION THROUGH THIMBLE AND SLEEVE

ONE-HANDED METHOD OF MEASURING
WITH A MICROMETER

USE LIGHT FINGERTIP PRESSURE ONLY

MAGNIFIED SECTION
THROUGH THE THREAD

SLEEVE

SCREW

FOR GREATER ACCURACY THE THREAD
BEARS ON THE FLANKS ONLY

METRIC MICROMETER

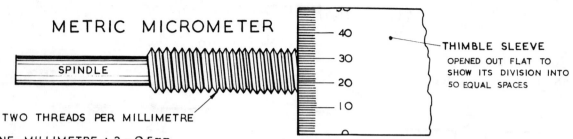

SPINDLE

TWO THREADS PER MILLIMETRE

ONE MILLIMETRE ÷ 2 = 0.5mm

THEREFORE ONE REVOLUTION OF THE SPINDLE, WHICH IS DRIVEN BY THE THIMBLE, MOVES IT LONGITUDINALLY THOUGH A DISTANCE OF 0.5mm. THUS IF THE THIMBLE IS DIVIDED INTO 50 EQUAL PARTS AS SHOWN, EACH DIVISION CAN BE READ AS 0.01mm OR ONE HUNDREDTH OF A MILLIMETRE

THIMBLE SLEEVE
OPENED OUT FLAT TO SHOW ITS DIVISION INTO 50 EQUAL SPACES

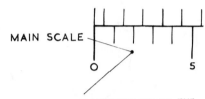

MAIN SCALE

THE MAIN SCALE IS DIVIDED BELOW THE DATUM LINE INTO MILLIMETRES. THESE ARE SUBDIVIDED ABOVE THE LINE INTO HALF MILLIMETRES   0.5mm

READING A MICROMETER

MAIN SCALE IS READ FROM THIS EDGE

MAIN SCALE

DATUM LINE

SECONDARY SCALE

SECONDARY SCALE READINGS ARE TAKEN FROM THE DATUM LINE

MAIN SCALE { 12
            { 0.5
SECONDARY SCALE 0.22

12.72 mm TOTAL READING

STANDARD 0-25mm HEAD (0-1")

VERNIER MICROMETER

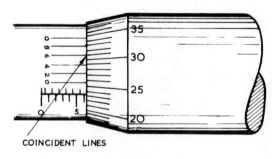

COINCIDENT LINES

MAIN SCALE — 6
THIMBLE SCALE — 0.23
VERNIER SCALE — 0.006

TOTAL READING — 6.236

10 SPACES ON THE VERNIER SCALE EQUAL
9 SPACES ON THE THIMBLE. SEE PAGE 24

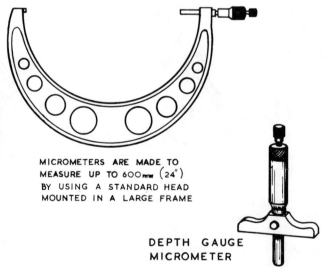

MICROMETERS ARE MADE TO MEASURE UP TO 600mm (24") BY USING A STANDARD HEAD MOUNTED IN A LARGE FRAME

DEPTH GAUGE MICROMETER

0-1" MICROMETER

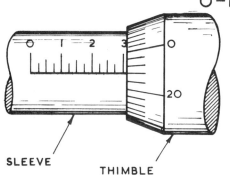

SLEEVE

THIMBLE

THE SLEEVE DATUM LINE IS DIVIDED INTO $\frac{1''}{10}$ SPACES OR 0·1". THESE ARE SUBDIVIDED INTO FOUR EQUAL SPACES OR 0·025", OR 25 THOUSANDTHS OF AN INCH

THE SPINDLE HAS 40 THREADS TO THE INCH. THUS IT ADVANCES 0·025" WITH EACH REVOLUTION

THE CIRCUMFERENCE OF THE THIMBLE IS DIVIDED INTO 25 EQUAL PARTS EACH OF WHICH IS READ AS ·001" OR ONE THOUSANDTH OF AN INCH

HIGHEST FIGURE ON SLEEVE   =   ·3
FIGURE ON SLEEVE BELOW DATUM =   ·020
SPACES BETWEEN FIGURE AND DATUM =   ·002
TOTAL READING   = $\overline{0·322''}$

VERNIER HEIGHT GAUGE
(DUAL READING)

USED FOR ACCURATELY MEASURING HEIGHTS AND TESTING FOR PARALLEL

THE HARDENED KNIFE OR FINGER CAN BE USED TO SCRIBE A LINE IN MARKING OUT

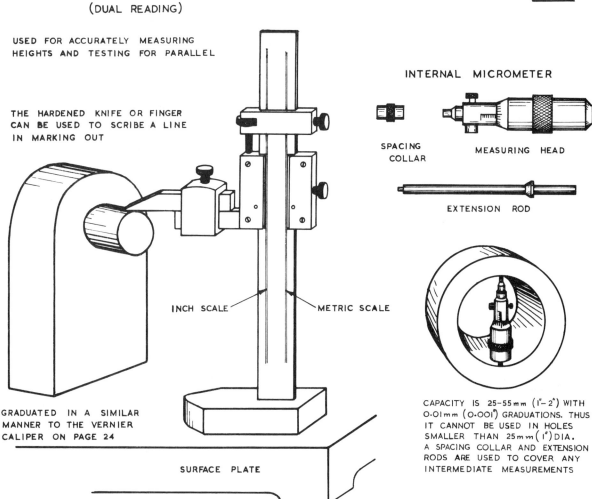

INCH SCALE   METRIC SCALE

GRADUATED IN A SIMILAR MANNER TO THE VERNIER CALIPER ON PAGE 24

SURFACE PLATE

INTERNAL MICROMETER

SPACING COLLAR

MEASURING HEAD

EXTENSION ROD

CAPACITY IS 25-55 mm (1"-2") WITH 0·01mm (0·001") GRADUATIONS. THUS IT CANNOT BE USED IN HOLES SMALLER THAN 25 mm (1") DIA. A SPACING COLLAR AND EXTENSION RODS ARE USED TO COVER ANY INTERMEDIATE MEASUREMENTS

VERNIER CALIPER

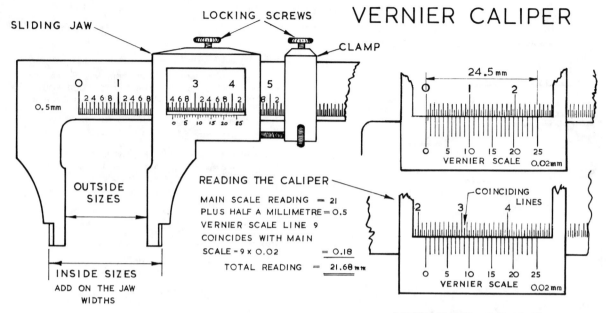

SLIDING JAW
LOCKING SCREWS
CLAMP
0.5mm

OUTSIDE SIZES

INSIDE SIZES
ADD ON THE JAW WIDTHS

24.5 mm
VERNIER SCALE   0.02mm

COINCIDING LINES
VERNIER SCALE   0.02 mm

READING THE CALIPER

MAIN SCALE READING = 21
PLUS HALF A MILLIMETRE = 0.5
VERNIER SCALE LINE 9
COINCIDES WITH MAIN
SCALE = 9 x 0.02 = 0.18
TOTAL READING = 21.68 mm

VERNIER SCALE

Each main scale division equals half a millimetre. If, therefore, the jaws are opened until the zero line on the vernier coincides with the first graduation past the zero on the main scale the jaws will have been opened half a millimetre (0.5 mm). Similarly, if the jaw is moved across the second space its total movement will have been 1 mm. The small engraved figures 2, 4, 6 and 8 denote mm. The space from the zero line to the large figure 1 equals one centimetre, or 10 mm. (It is customary in engineering to dimension whenever possible in millimetres only.)

The 25 divisions on the vernier scale occupy the same space as the 24.5 mm reading on the main scale. Therefore the magnitude of each vernier space or division will be 24.5 divided by 25, which equals 0.98 mm, or 0.02 mm shorter than two divisions on the main scale. In use, the clamp is secured first and the jaw is then accurately set by means of the fine adjustment screw.

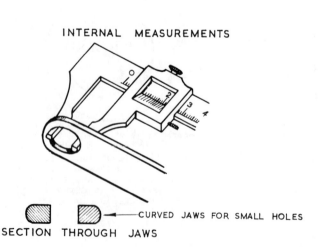

TAKING EXTERNAL MEASUREMENTS

INTERNAL MEASUREMENTS

CURVED JAWS FOR SMALL HOLES

SECTION THROUGH JAWS

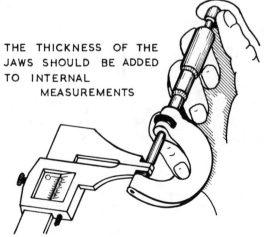

THE THICKNESS OF THE JAWS SHOULD BE ADDED TO INTERNAL MEASUREMENTS

VERNIER PROTRACTOR

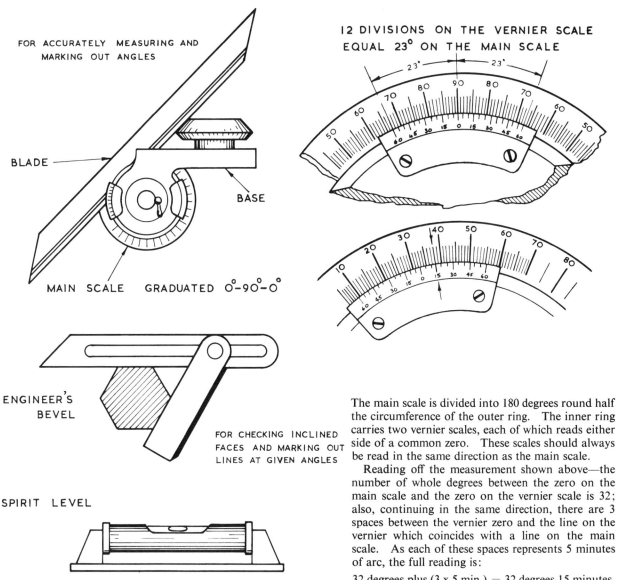

FOR ACCURATELY MEASURING AND
MARKING OUT ANGLES

BLADE

BASE

MAIN SCALE   GRADUATED 0°-90°-0°

ENGINEER'S
BEVEL

FOR CHECKING INCLINED
FACES AND MARKING OUT
LINES AT GIVEN ANGLES

SPIRIT LEVEL

STEEL STRAIGHT EDGE

BEVEL

CAST IRON STRAIGHT EDGE

STANDS ON THESE
FEET WHEN NOT
IN USE

FACE

12 DIVISIONS ON THE VERNIER SCALE
EQUAL 23° ON THE MAIN SCALE

The main scale is divided into 180 degrees round half the circumference of the outer ring. The inner ring carries two vernier scales, each of which reads either side of a common zero. These scales should always be read in the same direction as the main scale.

Reading off the measurement shown above—the number of whole degrees between the zero on the main scale and the zero on the vernier scale is 32; also, continuing in the same direction, there are 3 spaces between the vernier zero and the line on the vernier which coincides with a line on the main scale. As each of these spaces represents 5 minutes of arc, the full reading is:

32 degrees plus (3 x 5 min.) = 32 degrees 15 minutes.

SPIRIT LEVEL A spirit level is used for levelling machinery and also for setting up irregular work for marking out when some part of the work has to be horizontal. Spirit levels are often incorporated in the protractor and square heads of the combination sets, thus facilitating the setting up and checking of vertical and inclined faces as well as of horizontals.

STRAIGHT EDGE These are of two types: for small work, a hardened and tempered carbon steel strip with a bevel machined along one long edge; for larger work, an iron casting, ribbed for strength and with a rather thicker edge. In use they are placed against the surface to be tested and then checked against the light.

GAUGES

Slip gauges are rectangular blocks of hardened tool steel which have been ground and lapped to accurate sizes. The faces are so smooth that two gauges will cling together when they have been cleaned. A standard set of these gauges contains from 45 to 86 pieces, covering a range from 2.00 mm to 300 mm in steps of 0.001 mm (0.1″ to 12″ in steps of 0.001″). By using combinations of these blocks a wide range of dimensions can be built up. These are most often used for setting other gauges to accurate dimensions.

The dial indicator consists of a spring loaded plunger geared to a dial needle. The dial, which is commonly graduated in hundredths of a millimetre (or thousandths of an inch) is set by moving the outer knurled ring. The needle is set by means of the adjusting screw. The dial indicator is set to the required height on the appropriate slip gauges and then the work is passed underneath the plunger. The movement of the needle measures off the variation in size between the work and the set dimension.

SINE BAR

AN ACCURATE MEANS OF CHECKING TAPERS AND ANGLES

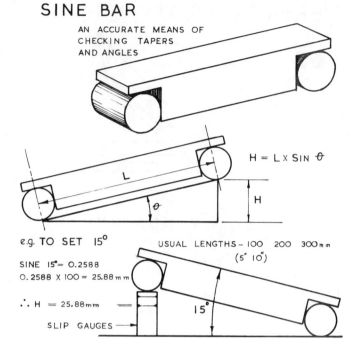

$H = L \times \sin \theta$

e.g. TO SET 15°

SINE 15° = 0.2588

0.2588 × 100 = 25.88 mm

∴ H = 25.88mm

SLIP GAUGES →

USUAL LENGTHS – 100   200   300 mm
(5″ 10″)

COMBINATION SET

USED IN NUMEROUS MARKING OUT AND MEASURING OPERATIONS

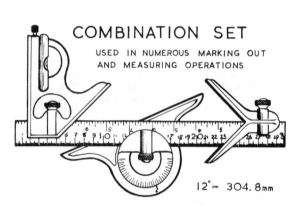

12″ = 304.8mm

USED AS A TRY SQUARE

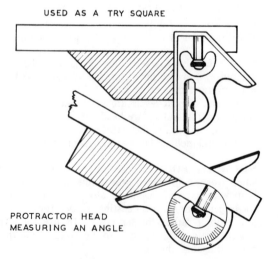

PROTRACTOR HEAD MEASURING AN ANGLE

SLIP GAUGES IN HOLDER

DIAL GAUGE OR 'CLOCK'

FOR RAPIDLY CHECKING HEIGHT FLATNESS AND ECCENTRICITY

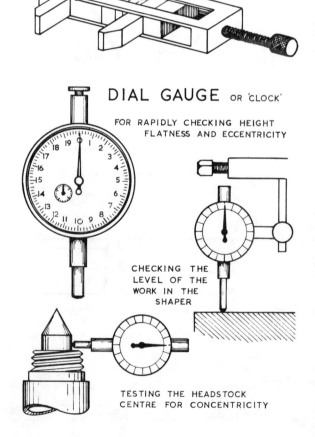

CHECKING THE LEVEL OF THE WORK IN THE SHAPER

TESTING THE HEADSTOCK CENTRE FOR CONCENTRICITY

Specially made gauges are widely used in mass production work to facilitate the checking of dimensions. The degree of accuracy of all gauges is determined, and varies with the type of work that is to be checked.

Plug and ring gauges test holes and shafts and are either 'standard' for measuring one dimension only, or 'limit' for maintaining size between upper and lower tolerances.

Snap gauges and caliper-type limit gauges also test overall size and in addition may be used to test for out of roundness.

Almost all gauges are made from tool steel, hardened and tempered to resist wear, and surface ground and lapped to close limits and a high surface finish.

LIMIT PLUG GAUGE DOUBLE-ENDED
FOR CHECKING HOLE SIZES

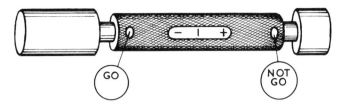

STANDARD RING GAUGE

FOR CHECKING SHAFT SIZES

THREADED PLUG AND RING GAUGES ARE USED FOR TESTING INTERNAL AND EXTERNAL SCREW THREADS

ADJUSTABLE LIMIT GAUGE

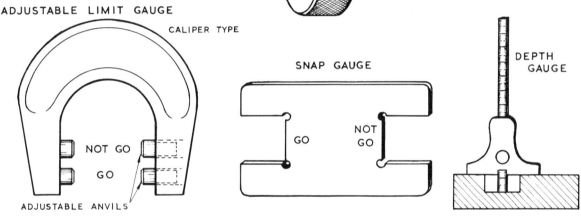

CALIPER TYPE

NOT GO

GO

ADJUSTABLE ANVILS

SNAP GAUGE

GO   NOT GO

DEPTH GAUGE

STANDARD WIRE GAUGE (S W G) BIRMINGHAM WIRE GAUGE (BWG) AND THE ZINC GAUGE (ZG) ARE OBSOLETE. IN FUTURE, THICKNESS OF METAL SHEET AND WIRE DIAMETERS WILL ALL BE SPECIFIED IN MILLIMETRES

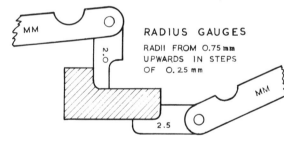

RADIUS GAUGES

RADII FROM 0.75 mm UPWARDS IN STEPS OF 0.25 mm

PROTRACTOR

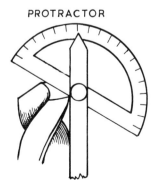

SCREW PITCH GAUGE

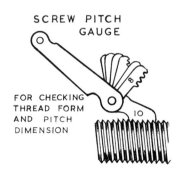

FOR CHECKING THREAD FORM AND PITCH DIMENSION

FEELER GAUGE

FOR MEASURING GAPS BETWEEN COMPONENTS.
BLADE THICKNESS IS MARKED IN HUNDREDTHS OF A MILLIMETRE

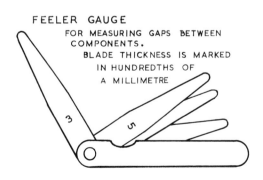

HOW TO FILE

FILING HINTS

1 Place the work low in the vice and parallel with the vice top

2 Take up a comfortable position, not too close to the work nor too far from it, and with the weight of the body balanced evenly on both feet.

3 Keep the shoulder and elbow joints free and easy moving. The wrist which is behind the file handle must be kept rigid to maintain the file in a flat position.

4 Apply pressure on the forward stroke, easing the pressure and lifting very slightly on the return stroke, remembering that the file cuts on the forward stroke only.

5 To produce a flat surface, the file should be used diagonally across the work, changing direction frequently.

6 Use the full length of the file and cover a large part of the work at each stroke.

7 Care should be taken to prevent files rubbing the hardened vice jaws as file teeth are brittle and easily broken. Files should be protected from impact with each other and with other hardened tools.

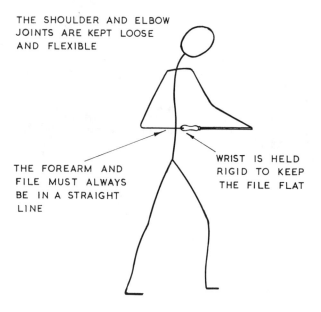

THE SHOULDER AND ELBOW JOINTS ARE KEPT LOOSE AND FLEXIBLE

THE FOREARM AND FILE MUST ALWAYS BE IN A STRAIGHT LINE

WRIST IS HELD RIGID TO KEEP THE FILE FLAT

WEIGHT BALANCED EVENLY ON BOTH FEET

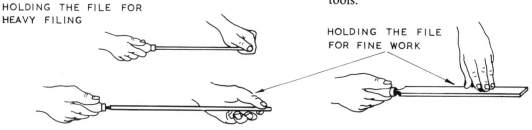

HOLDING THE FILE FOR HEAVY FILING

HOLDING THE FILE FOR FINE WORK

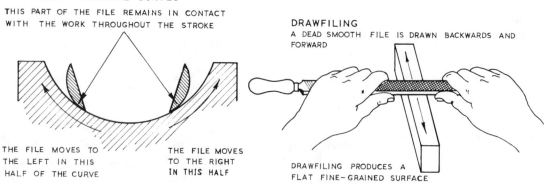

FILING INTERNAL CURVES

THIS PART OF THE FILE REMAINS IN CONTACT WITH THE WORK THROUGHOUT THE STROKE

THE FILE MOVES TO THE LEFT IN THIS HALF OF THE CURVE

THE FILE MOVES TO THE RIGHT IN THIS HALF

DRAWFILING

A DEAD SMOOTH FILE IS DRAWN BACKWARDS AND FORWARD

DRAWFILING PRODUCES A FLAT FINE-GRAINED SURFACE

FILE TEETH

ROUGH CUT

BASTARD CUT

SECOND CUT

SMOOTH CUT

DEAD SMOOTH

The number of teeth per 25 mm (1″) of cutting length varies not only with the cut but also in proportion to the length of the file. Thus a 150 mm (6″) second-cut file will have more teeth over a similar length than has a 250 mm (10″) second-cut file.

The choice of file is decided by the size and shape of the work. Bastard and rough cuts remove more metal, the smooth cuts less, but the latter produce a finer finish and greater accuracy. Files are specified by length, cut and section, the commonest probably being the 250 mm (10″) second-cut hand file. A file will last longer if it is used first on soft metals and also if care is taken to preserve the brittle teeth from impact damage.

Rifflers are small double ended files about 150 mm (6″) in length, similar in section to the standard files. They are used for the finishing of fine surfaces and shaping intricate work where little material needs to be removed.

ENLARGED CROSS SECTION OF FILE

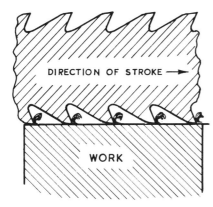

DIRECTION OF STROKE →

WORK

SINGLE-CUT FILE

65° TO 70°

DOUBLE-CUT FILE

USED FOR GENERAL WORK

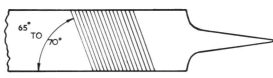

70°   45°

PINNING
THIS IS CAUSED BY SOFT METALS CLOGGING THE FILE TEETH AND SCRATCHING THE SURFACE OF THE WORK.

THE PINS ARE REMOVED WITH A FILE CARD (WIRE BRUSH) OR A BRASS ROD AS SHOWN

CHALK RUBBED INTO THE TEETH PREVENTS PINNING

FILES

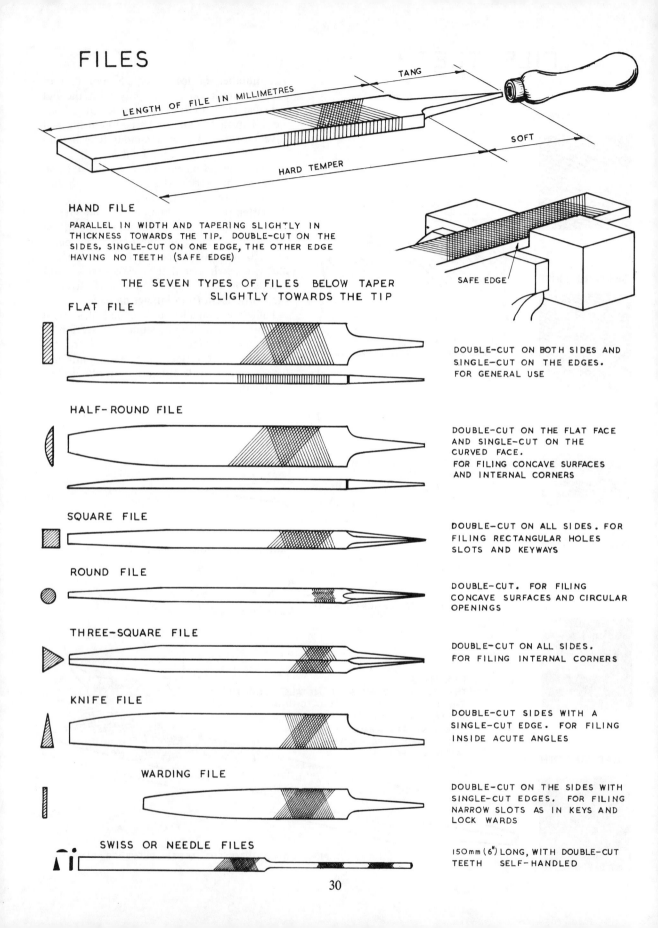

LENGTH OF FILE IN MILLIMETRES

TANG

SOFT

HARD TEMPER

HAND FILE

PARALLEL IN WIDTH AND TAPERING SLIGHTLY IN THICKNESS TOWARDS THE TIP. DOUBLE-CUT ON THE SIDES, SINGLE-CUT ON ONE EDGE, THE OTHER EDGE HAVING NO TEETH (SAFE EDGE)

SAFE EDGE

THE SEVEN TYPES OF FILES BELOW TAPER SLIGHTLY TOWARDS THE TIP

FLAT FILE

DOUBLE-CUT ON BOTH SIDES AND SINGLE-CUT ON THE EDGES. FOR GENERAL USE

HALF-ROUND FILE

DOUBLE-CUT ON THE FLAT FACE AND SINGLE-CUT ON THE CURVED FACE. FOR FILING CONCAVE SURFACES AND INTERNAL CORNERS

SQUARE FILE

DOUBLE-CUT ON ALL SIDES. FOR FILING RECTANGULAR HOLES SLOTS AND KEYWAYS

ROUND FILE

DOUBLE-CUT. FOR FILING CONCAVE SURFACES AND CIRCULAR OPENINGS

THREE-SQUARE FILE

DOUBLE-CUT ON ALL SIDES. FOR FILING INTERNAL CORNERS

KNIFE FILE

DOUBLE-CUT SIDES WITH A SINGLE-CUT EDGE. FOR FILING INSIDE ACUTE ANGLES

WARDING FILE

DOUBLE-CUT ON THE SIDES WITH SINGLE-CUT EDGES. FOR FILING NARROW SLOTS AS IN KEYS AND LOCK WARDS

SWISS OR NEEDLE FILES

150mm (6") LONG, WITH DOUBLE-CUT TEETH   SELF-HANDLED

COLD CHISELS

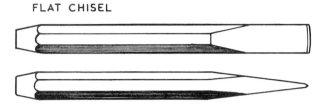

FLAT CHISEL

Cold chisels are made from carbon steel which has been hardened and tempered (to 280 °C purple oxide). The end which receives the hammer blow is forged and ground to a short taper to retard the mushrooming effect of frequent blows from a hard hammer face upon a softer chisel end. The cutting edges of the flat and the cross-cut chisels are ground to 60 degrees included angle. The edge is slightly convex to reduce the strain on the corners. When a chisel becomes too stubby through repeated grinding it is reforged to its original shape and then re-hardened and tempered.

In addition to the uses shown, the round-nose chisel is often used for 'drawing over' a centre in drilling, see page 66. The diamond point chisel is used for squaring out internal corners and for producing square holes following drilling.

CROSS-CUT OR CAPE CHISEL

ROUND-NOSE CHISEL

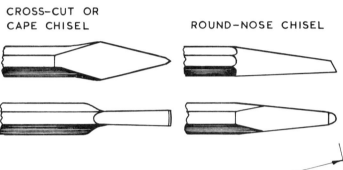

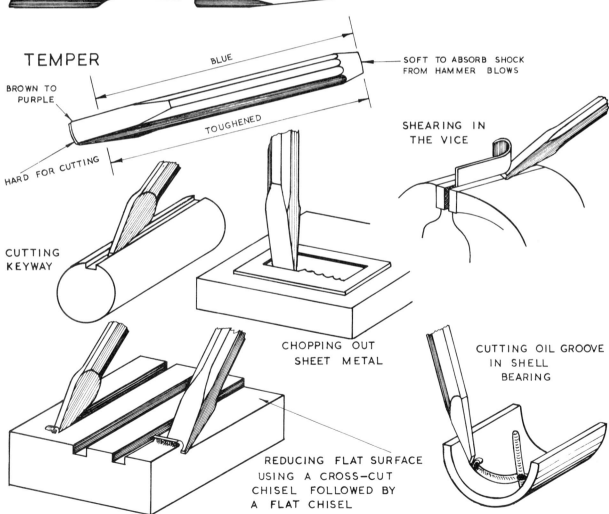

TEMPER

BLUE

SOFT TO ABSORB SHOCK FROM HAMMER BLOWS

BROWN TO PURPLE

TOUGHENED

HARD FOR CUTTING

SHEARING IN THE VICE

CUTTING KEYWAY

CHOPPING OUT SHEET METAL

CUTTING OIL GROOVE IN SHELL BEARING

REDUCING FLAT SURFACE USING A CROSS-CUT CHISEL FOLLOWED BY A FLAT CHISEL

HACKSAWS

Saw blades are specified by length and by the number of teeth cut in a standard distance along the cutting edge. The correct choice of pitch should ensure that three teeth are in contact with the section sawn. Blades should be inserted with the teeth pointing forward as the saw cuts on the forward stroke. Teeth are 'set' as shown to prevent the back of the blade binding in the sawcut. Flexible blades are soft for most of their width with only a narrow strip containing the teeth hardened and tempered. High speed steel blades are hardened and tempered throughout and retain their cutting edge longer. Little downward pressure is needed in sawing as the teeth are designed to pull themselves into the work. About 40 strokes per minute is the correct sawing speed.

Commonly used sizes	
250 mm (10″)	300 mm (12″)
18 24 32	Teeth per 25 mm of cutting length (teeth per inch)

For further details see B S 1919.

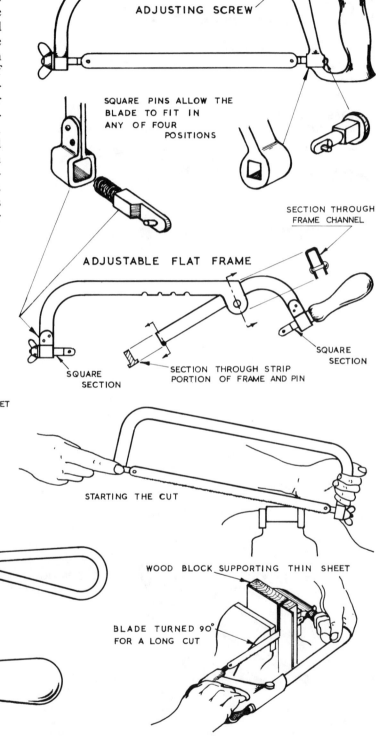

ADJUSTABLE TUBULAR HACKSAW FRAME

ADJUSTING SCREW

SQUARE PINS ALLOW THE BLADE TO FIT IN ANY OF FOUR POSITIONS

SECTION THROUGH FRAME CHANNEL

ADJUSTABLE FLAT FRAME

SQUARE SECTION

SECTION THROUGH STRIP PORTION OF FRAME AND PIN

SQUARE SECTION

STARTING THE CUT

WOOD BLOCK SUPPORTING THIN SHEET

BLADE TURNED 90° FOR A LONG CUT

COARSE TEETH SET

FINE TEETH SET

ENLARGED VIEW OF BLADE SHOWING THE SET AND ANGLE OF THE TEETH

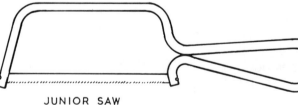

JUNIOR SAW

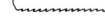

PAD HANDLE
WILL TAKE BROKEN BLADES

SCRAPERS

Scraping has two main functions: to produce a perfectly flat surface and an accurate fit between two mating surfaces. These aims are achieved by progressively removing the high spots from the surfaces. These high spots are shown up when one surface is slightly coated with a film of engineer's blue (Prussian blue oil paint) and then rubbed against the other. The surface plate is often used as a reference plane when preparing a flat surface. The first scraping is taken off in one constant direction. This is followed by a second pass over the work at right angles to the first scraping. Many machine beds and slideways are hand scraped and given a decorative finish by 'frosting'. Scraping is both slow and expensive and is now being superseded by surface grinding.

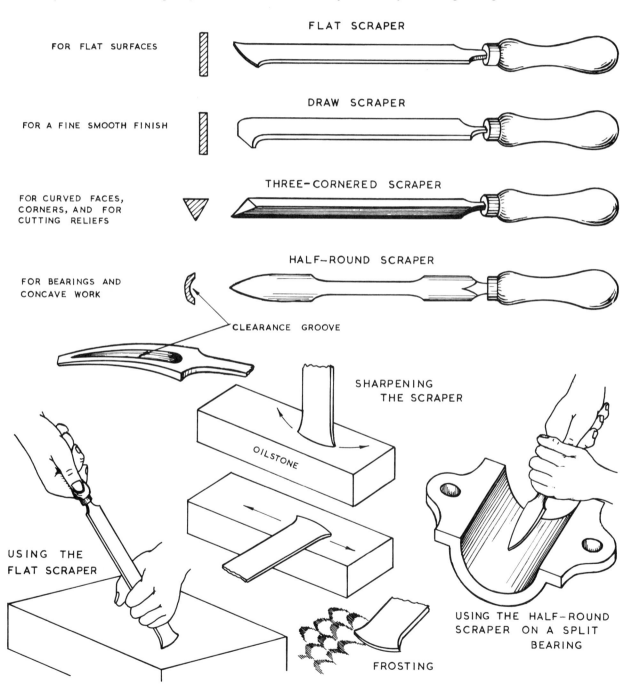

FOR FLAT SURFACES

FLAT SCRAPER

FOR A FINE SMOOTH FINISH

DRAW SCRAPER

FOR CURVED FACES, CORNERS, AND FOR CUTTING RELIEFS

THREE-CORNERED SCRAPER

FOR BEARINGS AND CONCAVE WORK

HALF-ROUND SCRAPER

CLEARANCE GROOVE

SHARPENING THE SCRAPER

OILSTONE

USING THE FLAT SCRAPER

FROSTING

USING THE HALF-ROUND SCRAPER ON A SPLIT BEARING

VICES

The parallel vice grips the work equally to the full depth of the jaws. The quick action trigger lowers the half-nut away from the screw so that the sliding jaw may be quickly adjusted. The vice body is made from cast iron which is strong in compression but fractures with shock and therefore should never be hammered. The buttress thread withstands heavy thrust in one direction yet unscrews easily in the opposite direction. Vices fitted with a rigid nut have square thread screws. The jaws are made of hardened steel with serrated surfaces to provide a firm grip. To prevent these serrations damaging soft work the jaws are covered with clamps made of lead, aluminium, or copper.

The Smith's leg vice is made of wrought iron with cast steel jaw inserts. It is used for heavy work, hammering and bending. Its main disadvantage is that the jaws move in an arc, thus providing a poor grip on wide work. The hand vice is used for holding metal whilst machining and is particularly useful for small work.

PARALLEL VICE

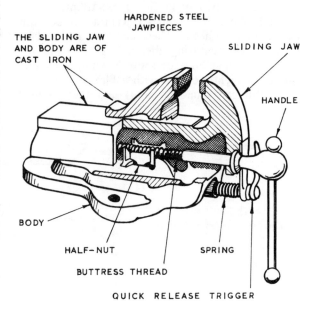

LEG VICE

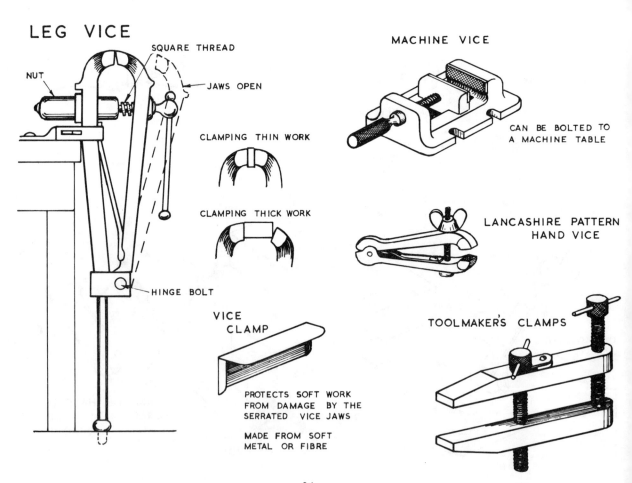

34

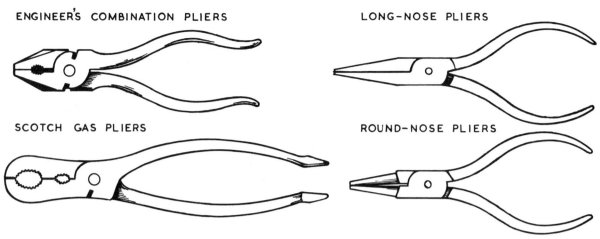

ENGINEER'S COMBINATION PLIERS

LONG-NOSE PLIERS

SCOTCH GAS PLIERS

ROUND-NOSE PLIERS

PLIERS There is a large variety of pliers, many designed for special purposes. The most commonly used are illustrated. They are made from carbon steel with hardened and tempered jaws.

HAMMERS Hammer heads are made from carbon steel. The faces are hardened and tempered whilst the eye is left soft to absorb shock. Handles are made from hickory or ash. Sizes are quoted as the weight of the head. 0.5 kg (1 lb) is used for general work and 0.75 kg (1½ lb) for forgework.

Only the centre of the hammer face should strike the work. The edges will bruise the work and they are liable to chip. Soft-faced hammers are being increasingly used to prevent this bruising.

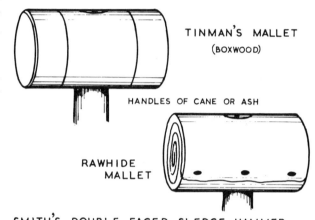

TINMAN'S MALLET
(BOXWOOD)

HANDLES OF CANE OR ASH

RAWHIDE
MALLET

SMITH'S DOUBLE-FACED SLEDGE-HAMMER

COMMON
SIZE IS 3.2 kg

ASH HANDLE

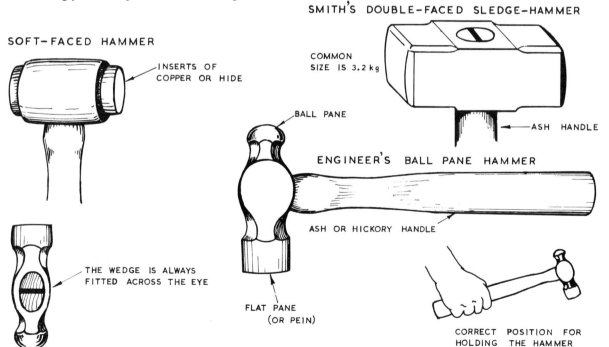

SOFT-FACED HAMMER

INSERTS OF
COPPER OR HIDE

THE WEDGE IS ALWAYS
FITTED ACROSS THE EYE

BALL PANE

ENGINEER'S BALL PANE HAMMER

ASH OR HICKORY HANDLE

FLAT PANE
(OR PEIN)

CORRECT POSITION FOR
HOLDING THE HAMMER

THREADING

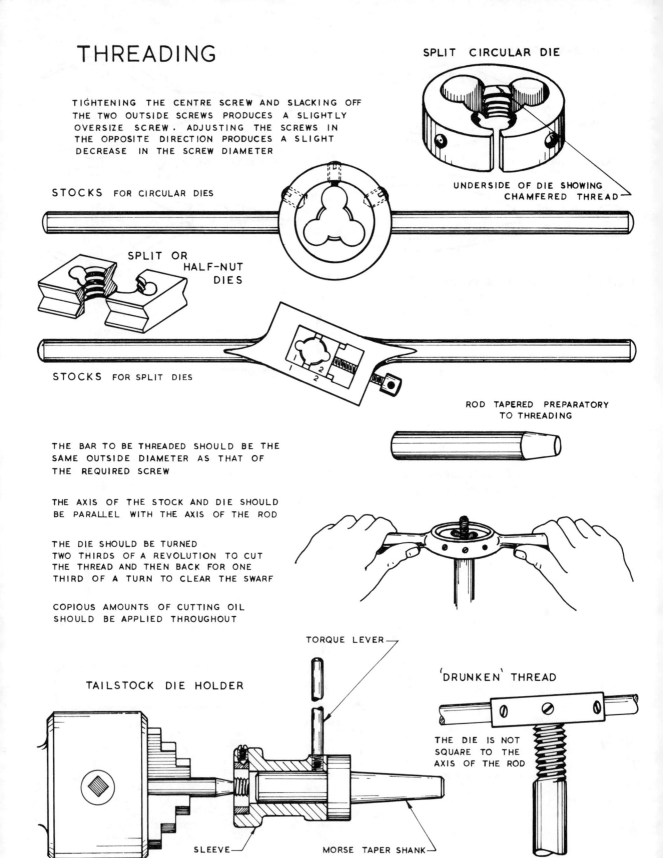

TIGHTENING THE CENTRE SCREW AND SLACKING OFF THE TWO OUTSIDE SCREWS PRODUCES A SLIGHTLY OVERSIZE SCREW. ADJUSTING THE SCREWS IN THE OPPOSITE DIRECTION PRODUCES A SLIGHT DECREASE IN THE SCREW DIAMETER

SPLIT CIRCULAR DIE

UNDERSIDE OF DIE SHOWING CHAMFERED THREAD

STOCKS FOR CIRCULAR DIES

SPLIT OR HALF-NUT DIES

STOCKS FOR SPLIT DIES

ROD TAPERED PREPARATORY TO THREADING

THE BAR TO BE THREADED SHOULD BE THE SAME OUTSIDE DIAMETER AS THAT OF THE REQUIRED SCREW

THE AXIS OF THE STOCK AND DIE SHOULD BE PARALLEL WITH THE AXIS OF THE ROD

THE DIE SHOULD BE TURNED TWO THIRDS OF A REVOLUTION TO CUT THE THREAD AND THEN BACK FOR ONE THIRD OF A TURN TO CLEAR THE SWARF

COPIOUS AMOUNTS OF CUTTING OIL SHOULD BE APPLIED THROUGHOUT

TORQUE LEVER

TAILSTOCK DIE HOLDER

'DRUNKEN' THREAD

THE DIE IS NOT SQUARE TO THE AXIS OF THE ROD

SLEEVE

MORSE TAPER SHANK

36

TAPPING

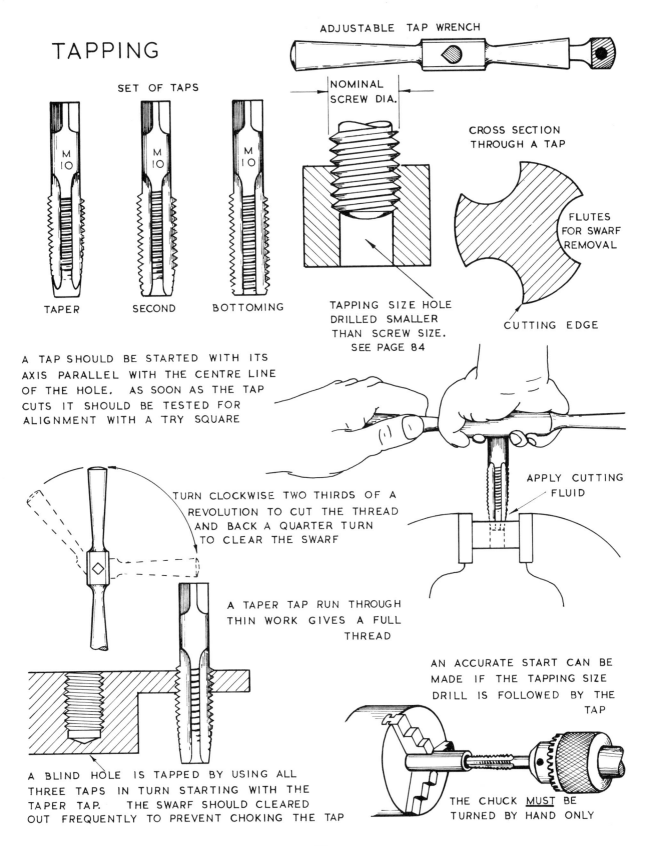

SET OF TAPS

ADJUSTABLE TAP WRENCH

NOMINAL SCREW DIA.

TAPER SECOND BOTTOMING

CROSS SECTION THROUGH A TAP

FLUTES FOR SWARF REMOVAL

CUTTING EDGE

TAPPING SIZE HOLE DRILLED SMALLER THAN SCREW SIZE. SEE PAGE 84

A TAP SHOULD BE STARTED WITH ITS AXIS PARALLEL WITH THE CENTRE LINE OF THE HOLE. AS SOON AS THE TAP CUTS IT SHOULD BE TESTED FOR ALIGNMENT WITH A TRY SQUARE

APPLY CUTTING FLUID

TURN CLOCKWISE TWO THIRDS OF A REVOLUTION TO CUT THE THREAD AND BACK A QUARTER TURN TO CLEAR THE SWARF

A TAPER TAP RUN THROUGH THIN WORK GIVES A FULL THREAD

AN ACCURATE START CAN BE MADE IF THE TAPPING SIZE DRILL IS FOLLOWED BY THE TAP

A BLIND HOLE IS TAPPED BY USING ALL THREE TAPS IN TURN STARTING WITH THE TAPER TAP. THE SWARF SHOULD CLEARED OUT FREQUENTLY TO PREVENT CHOKING THE TAP

THE CHUCK MUST BE TURNED BY HAND ONLY

SCREW THREADS

ISO METRIC THREAD   BS 3643

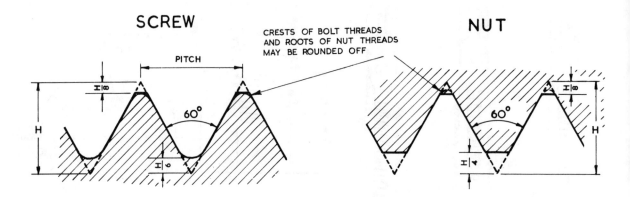

SCREW

NUT

PITCH

CRESTS OF BOLT THREADS
AND ROOTS OF NUT THREADS
MAY BE ROUNDED OFF

60°

60°

ISO METRIC SCREW THREADS BS 3643

The numerous thread systems used in the past have been superseded by the two systems recognised by the International Standards Organisation. The ISO metric thread will cover all metric systems whilst the ISO inch thread will cover usage of the current unified threads. Both use identical basic profiles designed so that nuts and screws make contact on the flanks only. Each is made in two series—Coarse pitch and Fine pitch—both with three classes of fits: Close, Medium and Free. The medium fit range will be the one most commonly used.

ISO METRIC MACHINE SCREWS BS 4183

This recommends four types of screw heads: pan-head, countersunk-head, raised countersunk-head and cheese-head. For preferred sizes see page 85. Screws are specified by material, type, diameter and length, e.g.

Brass cheese-head screw M13 x 10 mm.

UNIFIED SCREW THREADS BS 1580

The ISO unified thread has the same profile as the ISO metric thread shown above. However these two systems are not interchangeable owing to the differences between the diameters, one being expressed in inches and the other in millimetres.

BSW BSF THREADS

THESE ARE NOW OBSOLETE BEING REPLACED
BY THE ISO THREAD SYSTEMS

$D = .96 P$

$d = .64 P$

55°

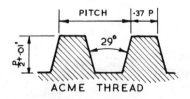

PITCH   ·37 P

29°

$\frac{P}{2} + .01$

ACME THREAD

TRANSMITS MOTION THROUGH
A DISENGAGING NUT.
LATHE LEAD SCREW

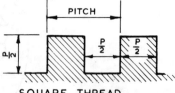

PITCH

$\frac{P}{2}$ $\frac{P}{2}$

$\frac{P}{2}$

SQUARE THREAD

FOR LOAD CARRYING PRESSES,
CAR JACKS, AND SOME VICES

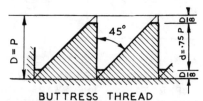

45°

$D = P$

$d = .75 P$

BUTTRESS THREAD

TRANSMITS PRESSURE IN ONE
DIRECTION ONLY. VICE SCREWS

SCREWS AND SPANNERS

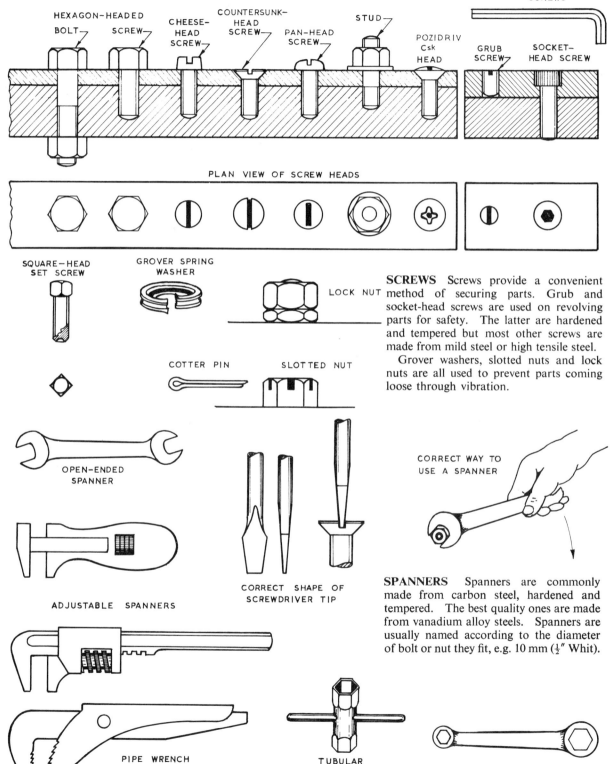

PLAN VIEW OF SCREW HEADS

'ALLEN KEY' SPANNER FOR SOCKET–HEAD SCREWS

HEXAGON–HEADED BOLT — SCREW —

CHEESE– HEAD SCREW —

COUNTERSUNK– HEAD SCREW —

PAN–HEAD SCREW —

STUD —

POZIDRIV Csk HEAD

GRUB SCREW —

SOCKET– HEAD SCREW

SQUARE–HEAD SET SCREW

GROVER SPRING WASHER

LOCK NUT

COTTER PIN   SLOTTED NUT

OPEN–ENDED SPANNER

ADJUSTABLE SPANNERS

CORRECT SHAPE OF SCREWDRIVER TIP

CORRECT WAY TO USE A SPANNER

PIPE WRENCH

TUBULAR BOX SPANNER

RING SPANNER

SCREWS Screws provide a convenient method of securing parts. Grub and socket-head screws are used on revolving parts for safety. The latter are hardened and tempered but most other screws are made from mild steel or high tensile steel.

Grover washers, slotted nuts and lock nuts are all used to prevent parts coming loose through vibration.

SPANNERS Spanners are commonly made from carbon steel, hardened and tempered. The best quality ones are made from vanadium alloy steels. Spanners are usually named according to the diameter of bolt or nut they fit, e.g. 10 mm ($\frac{1}{2}''$ Whit).

SOFT SOLDERING

Soldering is a method of joining metals by using an alloy having a lower melting point than the metals being joined, and which unites fully with them. The essentials for success are: (1) A clean well-fitting joint, (2) Clean flux of the right type, (3) A really hot, clean and well-tinned iron.

All except the smallest work should be pre-heated to the melting point of solder. In work of different sections, the heaviest will require the most heat. After heating, flux is applied and solder run into the joint from the soldering iron.

The finished work should be well washed in hot water to remove all traces of flux as many types of flux cause corrosion if allowed to remain on the work.

'Sweated joints' are those where the separate items are first coated with solder and then brought together and warmed until the solder runs through the joint.

Copper and brass solder easily, so does tinplate provided that the coating of tin is not destroyed by overheating. Mild steel needs thorough cleaning and flux needs to be constantly applied as oxides form rapidly at soldering temperature.

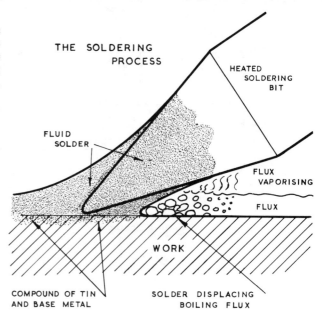

THE SOLDERING PROCESS

HEATED SOLDERING BIT

FLUID SOLDER

FLUX VAPORISING

FLUX

WORK

COMPOUND OF TIN AND BASE METAL

SOLDER DISPLACING BOILING FLUX

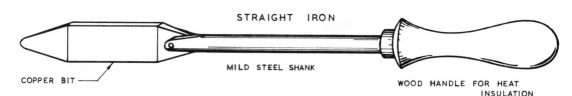

STRAIGHT IRON

COPPER BIT

MILD STEEL SHANK

WOOD HANDLE FOR HEAT INSULATION

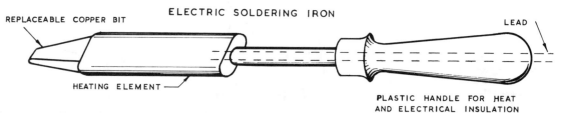

ELECTRIC SOLDERING IRON

REPLACEABLE COPPER BIT

LEAD

HEATING ELEMENT

PLASTIC HANDLE FOR HEAT AND ELECTRICAL INSULATION

TINNING THE BIT

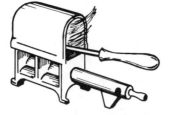

1. HEAT UNTIL THE GAS FLAME TURNS GREEN

2. SCOUR OFF THE DIRT FROM THE BIT WITH A WIRE BRUSH

3. QUICKLY DIP THE BIT IN AND OUT OF THE FLUX

4. RUB A STICK OF SOLDER OVER THE BIT, GIVING IT A THIN COATING ALL ROUND

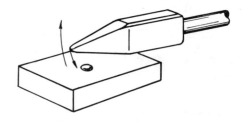

IF THE TINNED BIT IS TOUCHED ON A BEAD OF SOLDER AND QUICKLY RAISED AGAIN IT WILL IMMEDIATELY PICK UP THE SOLDER. IF NOT, IT SHOULD BE REHEATED AND CLEANED BY DIPPING IN FLUX

Soft solder is an alloy made from varying proportions of tin and lead. Some solders have a pasty stage, e.g. plumber's solder, which allows the joint to be 'wiped' whilst the solder is in a plastic state, whereas tinman's solder passes quickly from solid to liquid.

Fluxes are of two general types, zinc chloride and resin. Zinc chloride, or 'killed spirits' is a saturated solution of zinc in hydrochloric acid. This has excellent cleaning properties but necessitates thorough washing of the finished work or it will corrode the joint. This prohibits its use in electrical work where resin flux is exclusively used. Resin pastes are non-corrosive but have little cleaning action. The functions of a flux are:

Dissolving surface oxides;

Breaking down surface tension thus permitting the molten solder to flow more easily.

Soldering irons have copper bits because copper has an affinity for solder, has a high thermal capacity and is a good conductor of heat. Its main function is the transfer of heat from the soldering stove to the work.

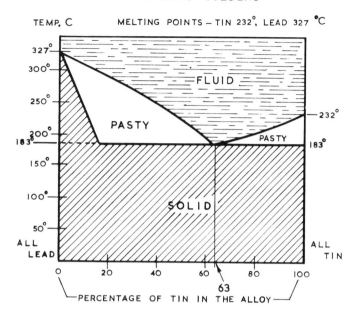

EQUILIBRIUM DIAGRAM OF
TIN LEAD SOLDERS

MELTING POINTS — TIN 232°, LEAD 327 °C

PERCENTAGE OF TIN IN THE ALLOY

CYCLE OF OPERATIONS IN SOLDERING

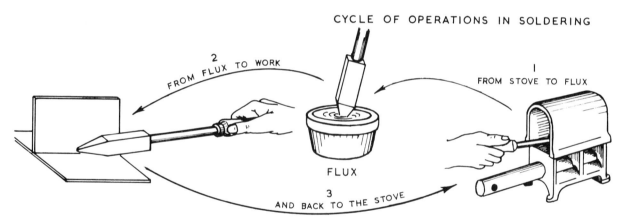

2 FROM FLUX TO WORK

1 FROM STOVE TO FLUX

3 AND BACK TO THE STOVE

FLUX

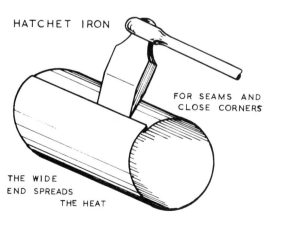

HATCHET IRON

FOR SEAMS AND CLOSE CORNERS

THE WIDE END SPREADS THE HEAT

METALS TO BE SOLDERED	FLUX REQUIRED	SOLDER ALLOYS		
		TIN	LEAD	OTHERS
ALUMINIUM	STEARIN	85	—	10 ZINC 5 ALUMINIUM
BRASS COPPER	ZINC CHLORIDE	65	35	
TINPLATE MILD STEEL	ZINC CHLORIDE	50	50	
ELECTRICAL WORK	RESIN	60	39.5	0.5 ANTIMONY
GALVANISED WORK ZINC	DILUTE HYDROCHLORIC ACID	50	50	
LEAD	TALLOW	30	70	
PEWTER BRITANNIA METAL	TALLOW GALLIPOLI OIL	25	25	50 BISMUTH

HARD SOLDERING

Hard soldering is a method of joining metals by using a molten alloy of greater strength than soft solder. This requires considerable heat which is supplied by a brazing torch which burns gas mixed with blown air. It is often necessary to secure the parts with iron wire to keep them in contact during heating. The work is surrounded by firebricks and then brought to red heat; the spelter wire is similarly heated, dipped in flux, applied to the work and then heated until the flux melts. This flows over the work clearing away the oxides, followed by the molten spelter. The heat should be maintained to allow the spelter to flow through the joint. Care has to be taken not to melt thin work whilst heating up heavier sections. Non-ferrous metals can have their oxides and spent fluxes removed by immersion in a bath made up from 1 part sulphuric acid and 7 parts water. This is termed 'pickling'. *Note.* When preparing this 'pickle' the acid must always be added to the water;

the reverse is highly dangerous. Immediately the work is removed from the acid bath it should be thoroughly washed under running water.

When the solder is composed of copper and zinc (brass), the process is termed 'brazing' and the solder 'spelter'. When silver is added to copper and zinc the process is termed 'silver soldering'. The addition of varying amounts of silver produces solders with a range of different melting points so that a particular solder may be selected to suit the requirements of the work in hand.

The fluxes are all made from calcined borax and are usually sold in paste or powdered form. Proprietory brands are available which have been developed to fuse at specific temperatures to match the range of solders.

COMPOSITION OF HARD SOLDERS

Silver	Copper	Zinc	Melting point °C
10	50	40	800
20	40	40	750
50	40	10	700

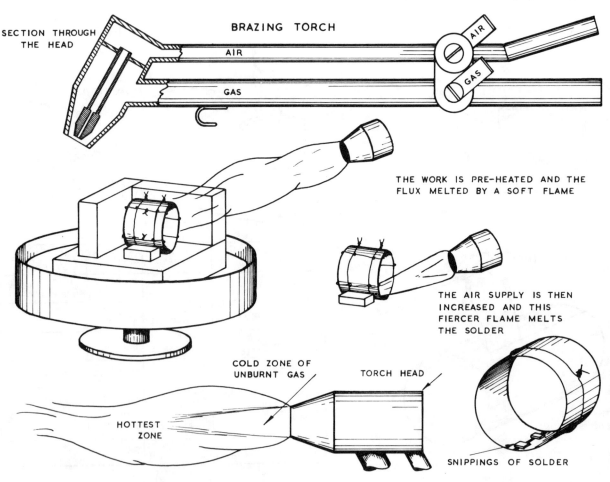

SECTION THROUGH THE HEAD

BRAZING TORCH

AIR

GAS

AIR

GAS

THE WORK IS PRE-HEATED AND THE FLUX MELTED BY A SOFT FLAME

THE AIR SUPPLY IS THEN INCREASED AND THIS FIERCER FLAME MELTS THE SOLDER

COLD ZONE OF UNBURNT GAS

TORCH HEAD

HOTTEST ZONE

SNIPPINGS OF SOLDER

SEAMING

Tinplate canisters, boxes and conical shapes have their edges joined together by various seams. The simplest is the lap joint, the laps being mitred when used on box corners, page 45. Canisters required to be watertight have their edges joined by the hooked or folded-and-grooved seam, page 43. This seam is set down so that the whole of the seam protrudes on one face of the work leaving the other face smooth. The folded seam around the base is usually set down to form a rim protecting the canister bottom from damage and wear. As tinplate is very thin and is frequently handled, the edges are rolled over to give a 'safe edge', page 43. Where extra strength is required, a length of wire is inserted in the rolled edge. It is customary to soft-solder all seams to seal them.

Note: All fold lines are marked with a pencil to avoid cutting through the protective coating of tin.

FALSE BEAD
OR SAFE EDGE

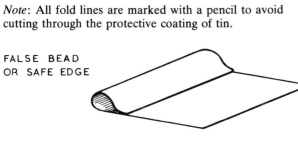

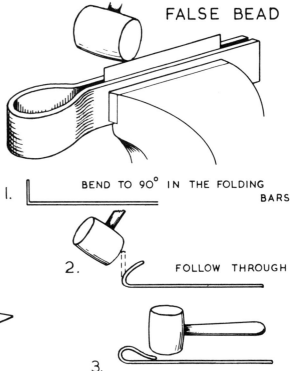

FALSE BEAD

1. BEND TO 90° IN THE FOLDING BARS

2. FOLLOW THROUGH

3. CLOSE DOWN THE EDGE

FOLDED AND GROOVED SEAM

1. BEND THE EDGE TO 90° AS IN FIG. 1 ABOVE

2. BEND OVER THE HATCHET

3. CLOSE DOWN OVER A STRIP OF STEEL

4. PULL THE EDGES TOGETHER AND CLOSE THEM WITH A HIDE MALLET

5. SET THE SEAM DOWN WITH A GROOVER OR A SEAM SET

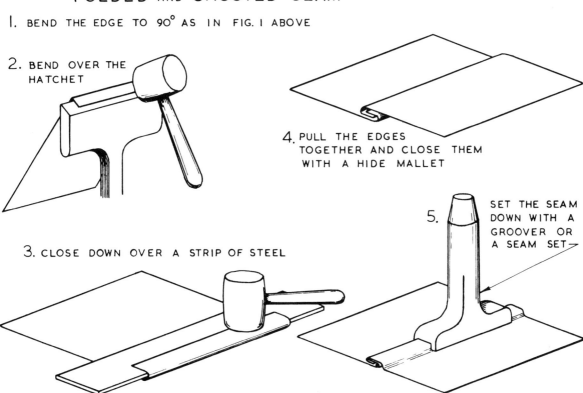

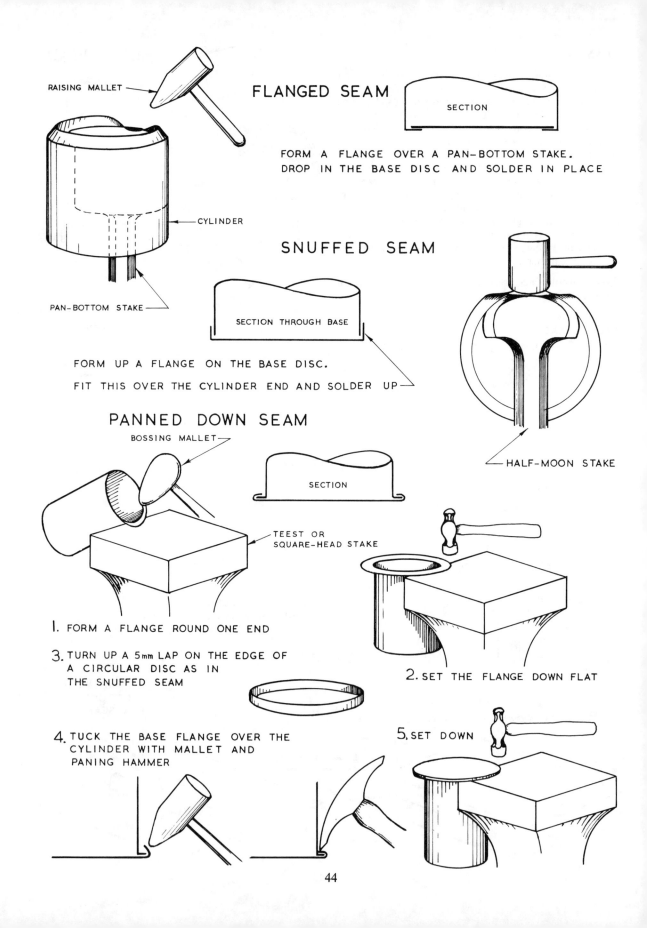

RAISING MALLET

FLANGED SEAM

SECTION

FORM A FLANGE OVER A PAN-BOTTOM STAKE.
DROP IN THE BASE DISC AND SOLDER IN PLACE

CYLINDER

SNUFFED SEAM

SECTION THROUGH BASE

PAN-BOTTOM STAKE

FORM UP A FLANGE ON THE BASE DISC.

FIT THIS OVER THE CYLINDER END AND SOLDER UP

HALF-MOON STAKE

PANNED DOWN SEAM

BOSSING MALLET

SECTION

TEEST OR
SQUARE-HEAD STAKE

1. FORM A FLANGE ROUND ONE END

3. TURN UP A 5mm LAP ON THE EDGE OF
   A CIRCULAR DISC AS IN
   THE SNUFFED SEAM

2. SET THE FLANGE DOWN FLAT

4. TUCK THE BASE FLANGE OVER THE
   CYLINDER WITH MALLET AND
   PANING HAMMER

5. SET DOWN

WIRED EDGES

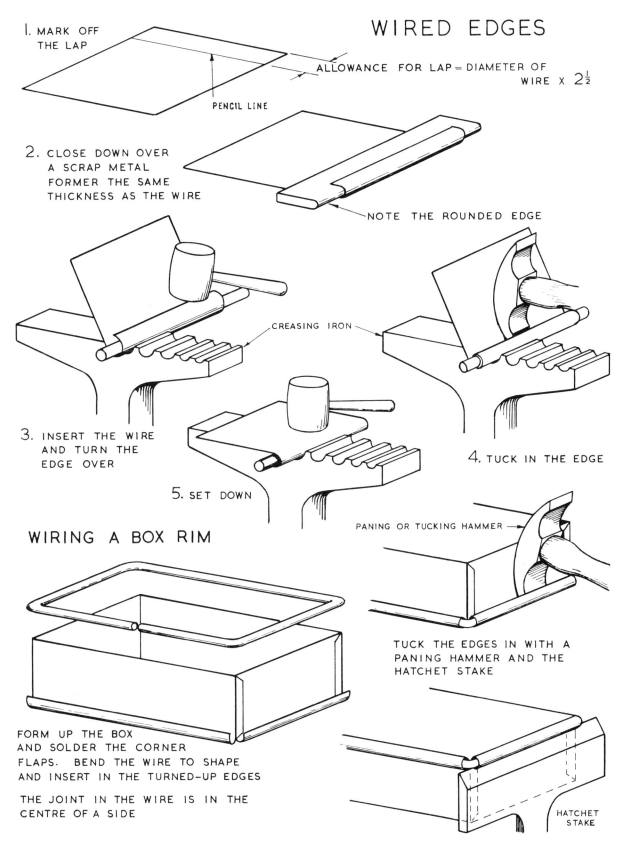

1. MARK OFF THE LAP

ALLOWANCE FOR LAP = DIAMETER OF WIRE x $2\frac{1}{2}$

PENCIL LINE

2. CLOSE DOWN OVER A SCRAP METAL FORMER THE SAME THICKNESS AS THE WIRE

NOTE THE ROUNDED EDGE

CREASING IRON

3. INSERT THE WIRE AND TURN THE EDGE OVER

4. TUCK IN THE EDGE

5. SET DOWN

PANING OR TUCKING HAMMER

WIRING A BOX RIM

TUCK THE EDGES IN WITH A PANING HAMMER AND THE HATCHET STAKE

FORM UP THE BOX AND SOLDER THE CORNER FLAPS. BEND THE WIRE TO SHAPE AND INSERT IN THE TURNED-UP EDGES

THE JOINT IN THE WIRE IS IN THE CENTRE OF A SIDE

HATCHET STAKE

DEVELOPMENTS

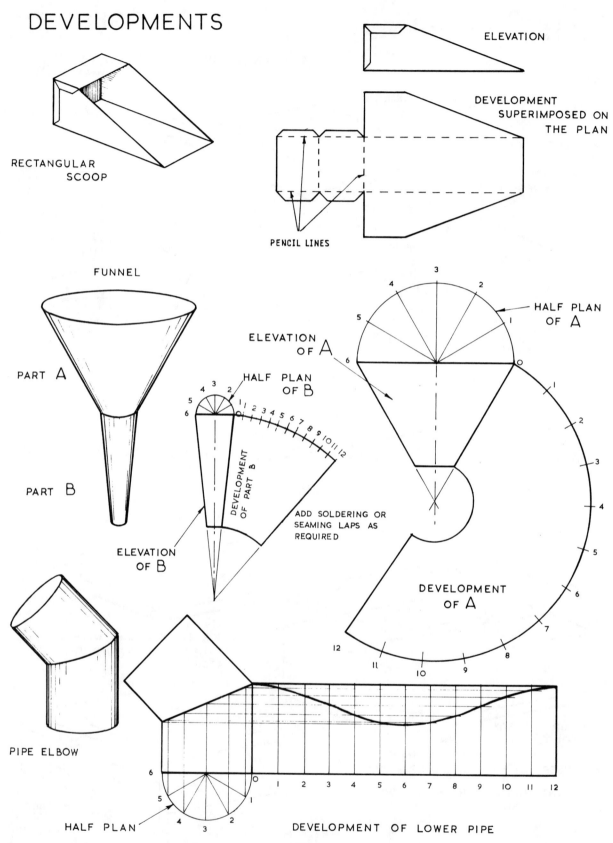

RECTANGULAR
SCOOP

ELEVATION

DEVELOPMENT
SUPERIMPOSED ON
THE PLAN

PENCIL LINES

FUNNEL

PART A

PART B

ELEVATION
OF A

HALF PLAN
OF A

HALF PLAN
OF B

DEVELOPMENT OF PART B

ADD SOLDERING OR
SEAMING LAPS AS
REQUIRED

ELEVATION
OF B

DEVELOPMENT
OF A

PIPE ELBOW

HALF PLAN

DEVELOPMENT OF LOWER PIPE

BENCH SHEARS

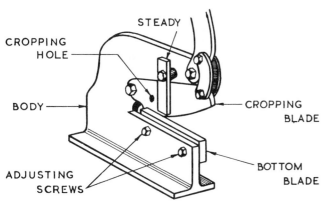

CROPPING HOLE

STEADY

BODY

CROPPING BLADE

ADJUSTING SCREWS

BOTTOM BLADE

BENCH SHEARS

Cutting is accomplished by a shearing action. The force is applied through a compound lever making it possible to cut sheet metal up to about 4 mm thick. The top blade, or cropper, is often provided with a hole for shearing rod. This can shear up to 10 mm dia. mild steel.

TINSNIPS

Tinsnips are of varying lengths, 200 mm and 250 mm being the ones in common use. Curved snips are for trimming inside curves and cylinders, straight snips for outside curves and straight lines, whilst universal snips will cut all the above. Work should always be held at right angles to the blade, and the points never closed on metal.

TINSNIPS

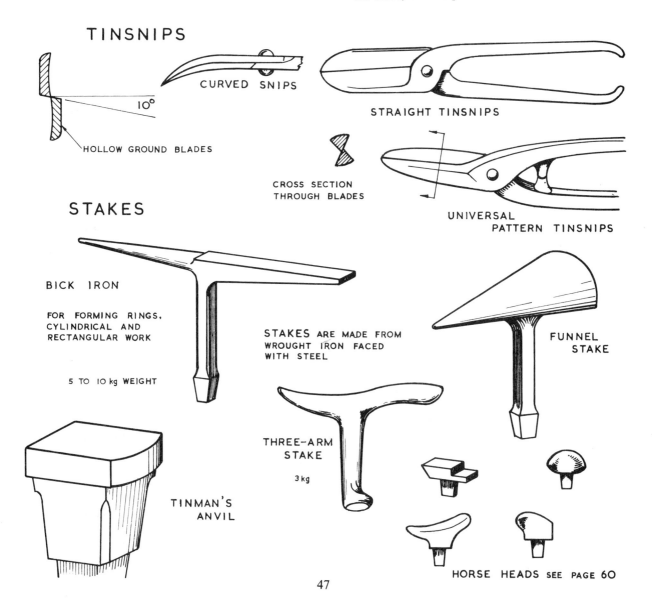

CURVED SNIPS

10°

HOLLOW GROUND BLADES

STRAIGHT TINSNIPS

CROSS SECTION THROUGH BLADES

UNIVERSAL PATTERN TINSNIPS

STAKES

BICK IRON

FOR FORMING RINGS, CYLINDRICAL AND RECTANGULAR WORK

5 TO 10 kg WEIGHT

STAKES ARE MADE FROM WROUGHT IRON FACED WITH STEEL

FUNNEL STAKE

THREE-ARM STAKE

3 kg

TINMAN'S ANVIL

HORSE HEADS SEE PAGE 60

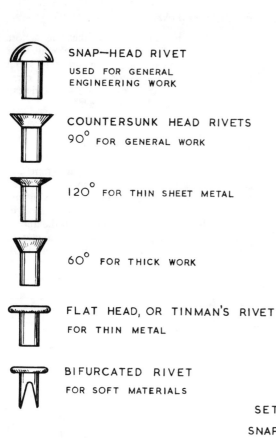

SNAP—HEAD RIVET
USED FOR GENERAL ENGINEERING WORK

COUNTERSUNK HEAD RIVETS
90° FOR GENERAL WORK

120° FOR THIN SHEET METAL

60° FOR THICK WORK

FLAT HEAD, OR TINMAN'S RIVET
FOR THIN METAL

BIFURCATED RIVET
FOR SOFT MATERIALS

RIVETING

Riveting is a simple way to join metal parts together. Rivets can form hinge pins in moving joints such as in tinsnips, or in rigid joints as in ship's plating. Rivets are made of soft iron for general engineering; aluminium alloy for aircraft work and soft aluminium or copper for non-metallic substances. Countersunk-heads are used where a smooth surface is required. A wide range of special rivets is available, mainly variations on the tubular rivet, for riveting from one side of the work only. This is done by a self-contained 'necked' dolly or a small explosive pellet, either of which expands and locks the 'blind' side of the rivet.

RIVETING DIMENSIONS

Diameter of rivet = 1.2 x thickness of one plate
Edge of hole to edge of plate
$\qquad$ = 1.5 x diameter of rivet
Distance between rivet centres
$\qquad$ = 3 x diameter of rivet
Length of shank projecting
$\qquad$ = Diameter of rivet

It is usual to drill all the holes in one plate and only one in the other, secure them with a rivet and complete the drilling.

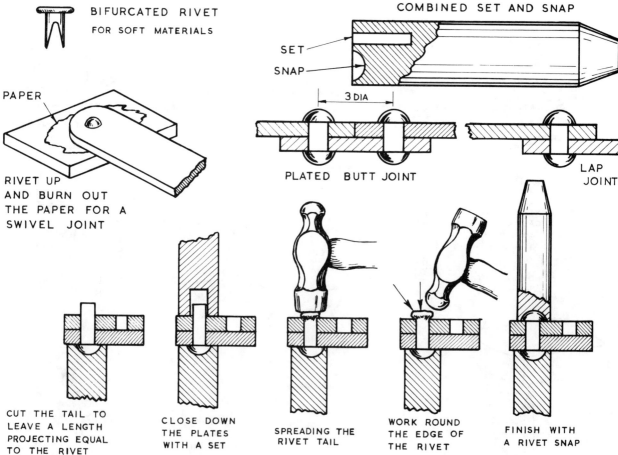

PAPER

RIVET UP AND BURN OUT THE PAPER FOR A SWIVEL JOINT

COMBINED SET AND SNAP

SET
SNAP

3 DIA

PLATED BUTT JOINT

LAP JOINT

CUT THE TAIL TO LEAVE A LENGTH PROJECTING EQUAL TO THE RIVET DIAMETER

CLOSE DOWN THE PLATES WITH A SET

SPREADING THE RIVET TAIL

WORK ROUND THE EDGE OF THE RIVET

FINISH WITH A RIVET SNAP

48

FORGING

Constant attention must be given to the fire to keep it clean, full and bright. Clinker should be removed before lighting up and when it reforms the air blast should be closed and the forge cooled a little to solidify the clinker, when it can be removed in one piece and the fire revived. Minimum air blast minimises the formation of clinker and oxidation of the work. The maintenance of a full fire will help protect the work from oxidation or 'burning'.

The anvil should always be treated with care. The face is made from hardened steel and should never be struck with the hammer as this causes chips of steel to break from the edges of both hammer and anvil, thus ruining both.

Suitably shaped tongs should be selected to fit the work. These should hold it securely to prevent its bouncing out of control from repeated hammer blows.

Care should be exercised in the use of the hammer. The minimum force only should be used and the flat face should strike squarely on the work as the edge of the hammer will produce heavy bruising on hot metal.

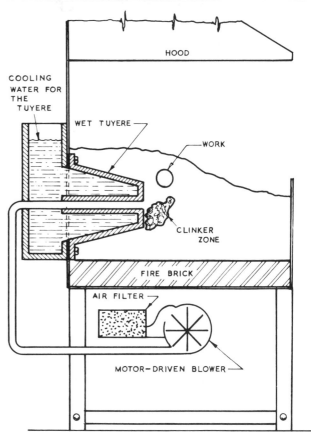

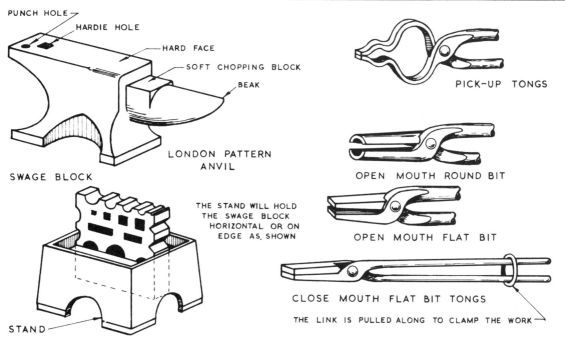

SWAGE BLOCK

LONDON PATTERN ANVIL

THE STAND WILL HOLD THE SWAGE BLOCK HORIZONTAL OR ON EDGE AS SHOWN

STAND

PICK-UP TONGS

OPEN MOUTH ROUND BIT

OPEN MOUTH FLAT BIT

CLOSE MOUTH FLAT BIT TONGS

THE LINK IS PULLED ALONG TO CLAMP THE WORK

DRAWING DOWN TO A POINT

DRAW DOWN TO A SHORT
SQUARE POINT

NOTE THE ANGLE
BETWEEN
WORK AND ANVIL FACE

THE HAMMER SQUEEZES
THE WORK ON TO THE
ANVIL FACE TO DRAW
OUT THE POINT

DRAW DOWN TO A
LONG SQUARE POINT

HAMMER DOWN THE CORNERS TO CHANGE THE POINT

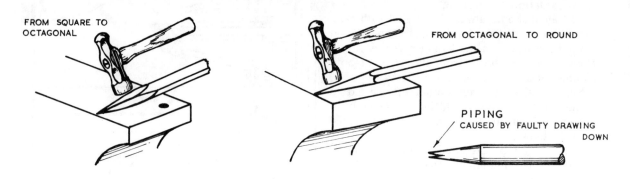

FROM SQUARE TO
OCTAGONAL

FROM OCTAGONAL TO ROUND

PIPING
CAUSED BY FAULTY DRAWING
DOWN

FORMING A LOOP

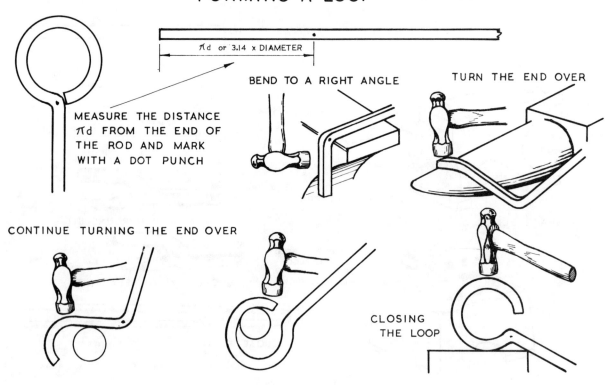

πd or 3.14 x DIAMETER

MEASURE THE DISTANCE
πd FROM THE END OF
THE ROD AND MARK
WITH A DOT PUNCH

BEND TO A RIGHT ANGLE

TURN THE END OVER

CONTINUE TURNING THE END OVER

CLOSING
THE LOOP

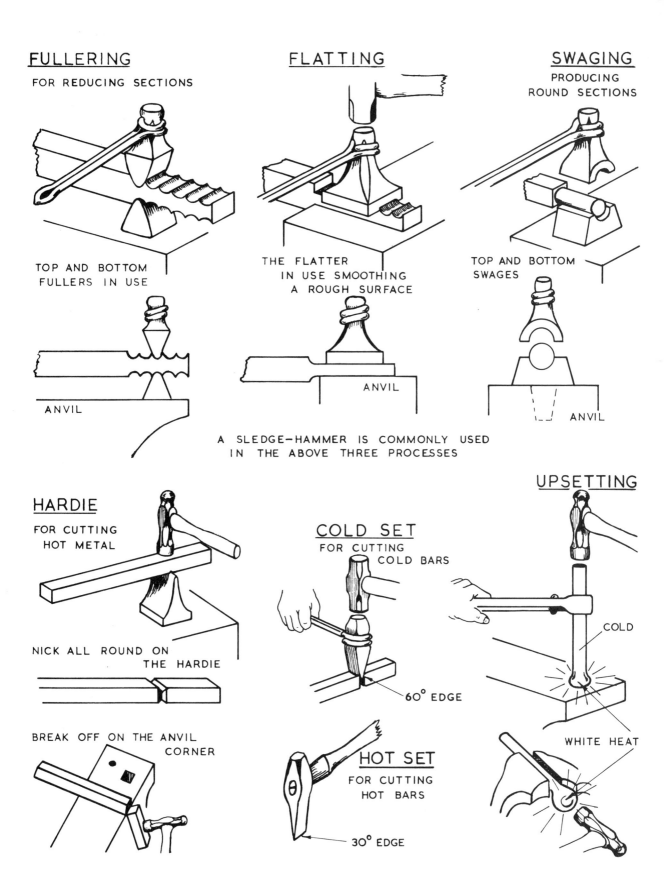

FULLERING
FOR REDUCING SECTIONS

TOP AND BOTTOM
FULLERS IN USE

ANVIL

FLATTING

THE FLATTER
IN USE SMOOTHING
A ROUGH SURFACE

ANVIL

SWAGING
PRODUCING
ROUND SECTIONS

TOP AND BOTTOM
SWAGES

ANVIL

A SLEDGE-HAMMER IS COMMONLY USED
IN THE ABOVE THREE PROCESSES

HARDIE
FOR CUTTING
HOT METAL

NICK ALL ROUND ON
THE HARDIE

BREAK OFF ON THE ANVIL
CORNER

COLD SET
FOR CUTTING
COLD BARS

60° EDGE

HOT SET
FOR CUTTING
HOT BARS

30° EDGE

UPSETTING

COLD

WHITE HEAT

SCROLLING AND TWISTING

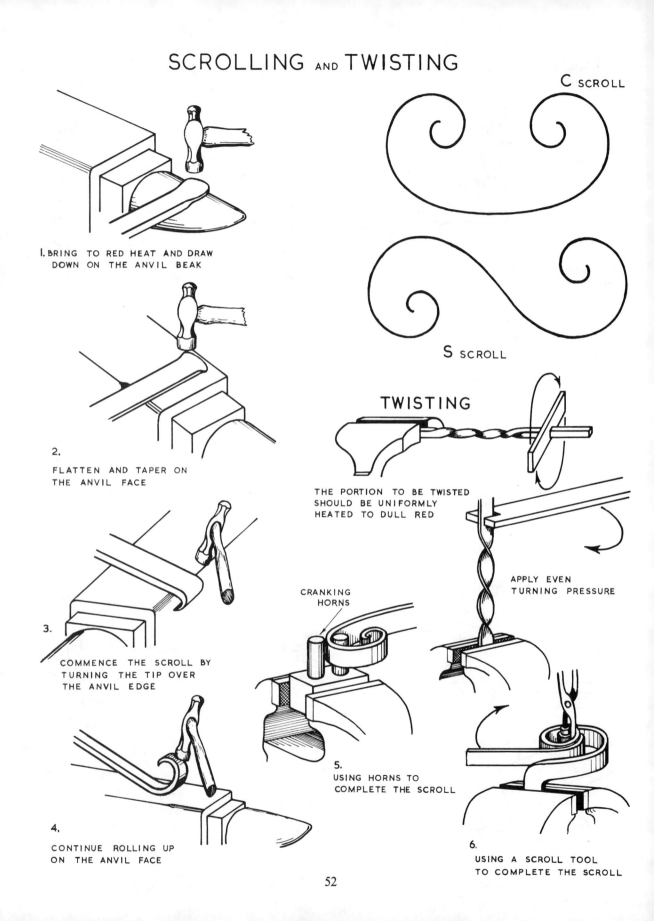

C SCROLL

1. BRING TO RED HEAT AND DRAW DOWN ON THE ANVIL BEAK

2.
FLATTEN AND TAPER ON THE ANVIL FACE

S SCROLL

TWISTING

THE PORTION TO BE TWISTED SHOULD BE UNIFORMLY HEATED TO DULL RED

APPLY EVEN TURNING PRESSURE

3.
COMMENCE THE SCROLL BY TURNING THE TIP OVER THE ANVIL EDGE

CRANKING HORNS

4.
CONTINUE ROLLING UP ON THE ANVIL FACE

5.
USING HORNS TO COMPLETE THE SCROLL

6.
USING A SCROLL TOOL TO COMPLETE THE SCROLL

FORGE WELDING

This is done by hammering the two parts together whilst at white heat. The workpieces are 'upset' to thicken them at the point which is to be welded and the contact surfaces are curved so that the weld can start from the centre, thus forcing the flux and dissolved oxide out of the joint as it is progressively closed. The whole welding operation, from withdrawing the metal from the fire through positioning on the anvil, fluxing and bringing the parts together and hammering to a unified mass, must be carried out rapidly and completed before there is any reduction from white heat. The welded joint can then be more slowly hammered to the final shape at a red heat.

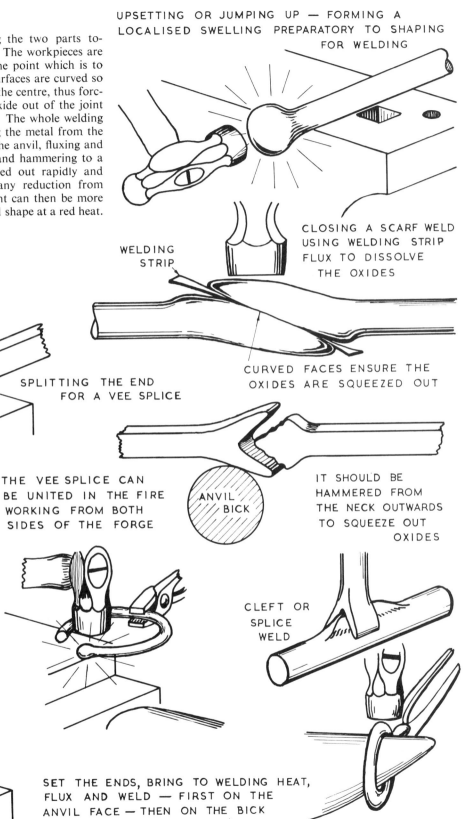

UPSETTING OR JUMPING UP — FORMING A LOCALISED SWELLING PREPARATORY TO SHAPING FOR WELDING

WELDING STRIP

CLOSING A SCARF WELD USING WELDING STRIP FLUX TO DISSOLVE THE OXIDES

CURVED FACES ENSURE THE OXIDES ARE SQUEEZED OUT

SPLITTING THE END FOR A VEE SPLICE

THE VEE SPLICE CAN BE UNITED IN THE FIRE WORKING FROM BOTH SIDES OF THE FORGE

ANVIL BICK

IT SHOULD BE HAMMERED FROM THE NECK OUTWARDS TO SQUEEZE OUT OXIDES

FORGING A RING

FORM AN OFFSET SCARF ON THE ENDS

CLEFT OR SPLICE WELD

SET THE ENDS, BRING TO WELDING HEAT, FLUX AND WELD — FIRST ON THE ANVIL FACE — THEN ON THE BICK

GAS WELDING

This is carried out by melting the edges of the work so that they run, or fuse, together. To ensure fusion right through the joint a small gap is left between the two pieces and, in addition, plates over 3 mm thick have their edges bevelled. This gap is closed up by a 'filler rod' which is melted simultaneously with the edges. The high temperature required is obtained by the combustion of acetylene in oxygen. These two gases are stored under pressure in separate cylinders and are drawn off through supply and safety valves. Gauges are fitted to indicate gas pressures both in the cylinders and in the feed pipes. The two gases enter the nozzle via a mixing chamber. The pressure in the feed pipes can be adjusted by valves and the rate of flow by a series of interchangeable nozzles having different apertures.

Students are strongly recommended to read *Safety in the Use of Compressed Gas Cylinders* and *Handbook of Instructions,* published by The British Oxygen Co. Ltd, Great West House, Brentford, Middlesex.

GAUGE TO INDICATE THE HOSELINE PRESSURE
0 — 2.1 bar
(0 – 30 lb/in²)

GAUGE TO INDICATE CYLINDER PRESSURE
0 — 175 bar
(0 – 2500 lb/in²)

REGULATING VALVE

RUBBER HOSE TO BLOWPIPE

NEEDLE VALVE TO OPEN THE CYLINDER

DANGER

WARNING NOTICE

NEVER USE OIL OR GREASE ON OXYGEN CONNECTORS

WELDING BLOWPIPES

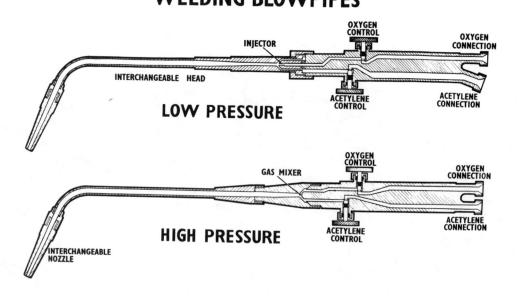

INJECTOR

OXYGEN CONTROL

OXYGEN CONNECTION

INTERCHANGEABLE HEAD

ACETYLENE CONTROL

ACETYLENE CONNECTION

LOW PRESSURE

GAS MIXER

OXYGEN CONTROL

OXYGEN CONNECTION

ACETYLENE CONTROL

ACETYLENE CONNECTION

INTERCHANGEABLE NOZZLE

HIGH PRESSURE

THE BRITISH OXYGEN COMPANY LTD.

LEFTWARD WELDING

In leftward welding the nozzle is held at about 65 degrees to the work and is traversed from right to left following a zig-zag path as shown below. The flame points towards and pre-heats the open uncompleted part of the joint. This is the method usually employed for welding metals up to about 5 mm thick.

RIGHTWARD WELDING

In rightward welding the nozzle is held at about 45 degrees to the work and is moved, with very little oscillating movement, from left to right. The flame thus points towards the completed part of the joint. This reduces the rate of cooling thereby inducing a more normal grain structure throughout the joint which lessens the liability of cracking in the weld.

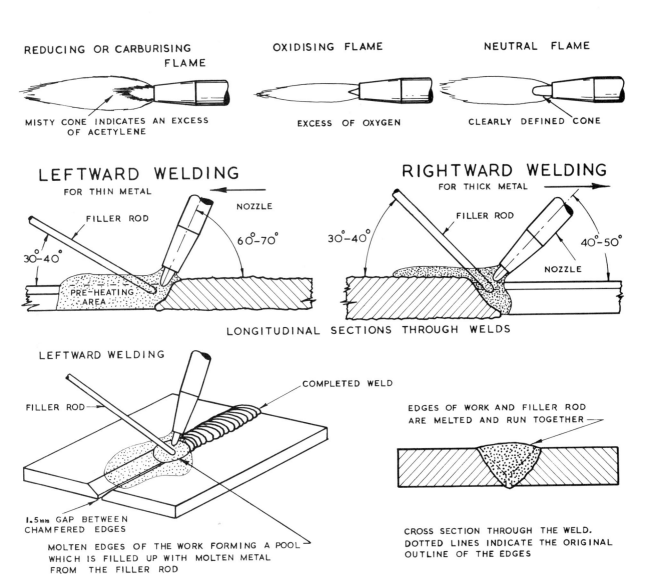

REDUCING OR CARBURISING FLAME

MISTY CONE INDICATES AN EXCESS OF ACETYLENE

OXIDISING FLAME

EXCESS OF OXYGEN

NEUTRAL FLAME

CLEARLY DEFINED CONE

LEFTWARD WELDING

FOR THIN METAL

FILLER ROD

NOZZLE

60°–70°

30°–40°

PRE-HEATING AREA

RIGHTWARD WELDING

FOR THICK METAL

FILLER ROD

30°–40°

40°–50°

NOZZLE

LONGITUDINAL SECTIONS THROUGH WELDS

LEFTWARD WELDING

FILLER ROD

COMPLETED WELD

1.5mm GAP BETWEEN CHAMFERED EDGES

MOLTEN EDGES OF THE WORK FORMING A POOL WHICH IS FILLED UP WITH MOLTEN METAL FROM THE FILLER ROD

EDGES OF WORK AND FILLER ROD ARE MELTED AND RUN TOGETHER

CROSS SECTION THROUGH THE WELD. DOTTED LINES INDICATE THE ORIGINAL OUTLINE OF THE EDGES

HARDENING

Before hardening a tool it is customary to normalise it. Normalising relieves internal stresses resulting from previous treatment and refines the grain structure. It is done by heating the steel above its upper critical temperature and allowing it to cool in air.

The tool is then hardened by heating it to a cherry red colour for about half the length from the cutting edge and immediately quenching in a bath of oil, brine, or tepid water. (Quenching in cold water is too severe and can cause surface cracks). The tool should be plunged vertically to prevent distortion and kept moving to prevent uneven cooling caused by the formation of steam. The tool will then be extremely hard. The higher the carbon content the harder the steel.

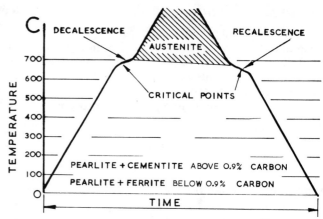

STRUCTURAL CHANGE WHEN HEATED

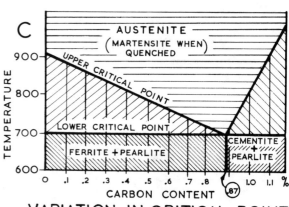

VARIATION IN CRITICAL POINTS

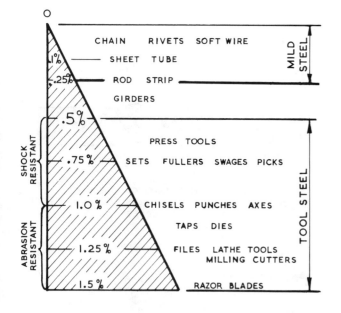

CARBON CONTENT IN STEELS

Case Hardening (Carburising)

Mild steel cannot be hardened as it does not contain sufficient carbon. It can be made to absorb carbon, which in practice penetrates to about 1 mm and this carbon rich skin can then be hardened. Usually all the forming operations are completed and then the item is brought to red heat and plunged into a carbonaceous material, commonly powdered charcoal produced from charred animal bones and skins. This adheres to the metal. The process is repeated a few times to obtain a good penetration of carbon. It is finally quenched from red heat giving a hard casing over a soft core.

TEMPERING

This reduces the hardness and brittleness of hardened tool steel, bringing it to the correct degree of toughness required. The tool is thoroughly polished along one face so as to show up the oxide colours. Heat is then applied well back from the cutting edge. At about 235 °C the polished steel will be covered with a pale yellow oxide. As the temperature rises the oxide layer thickens and changes colour from straw to brown and then to purple and finally to blue. These colours creep along the tool as heat is applied. When the required colour reaches the tip the tool is quenched in water.

Point Hardening and Tempering. This is a quick method for small tools. The tool is heated to cherry-red for about half its length. About 50 mm from the tip is quenched, and therefore hardened. This is quickly polished on a sandstone or emery block. The residual heat from the unquenched shank will then travel back to the tip and when the required colour is attained the whole tool is quenched.

Annealing is heating steel slightly above the upper critical point and cooling slowly away from air, usually in hot ashes. This relieves stresses, refines the grain structure and softens the steel.

1. POLISH THE LOWER HALF OF THE TOOL WITH EMERY CLOTH

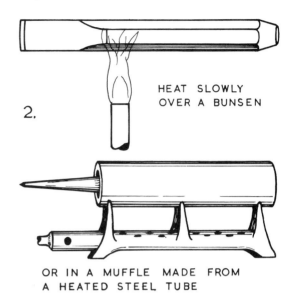

HEAT SLOWLY OVER A BUNSEN

2.

OR IN A MUFFLE MADE FROM A HEATED STEEL TUBE

OR IN A SAND TRAY

NOTE — THE TIP SHOULD BE HEATED INDIRECTLY THROUGH THE SHANK

3. QUENCH IN COLD WATER IMMEDIATELY THE CORRECT OXIDE COLOUR APPEARS

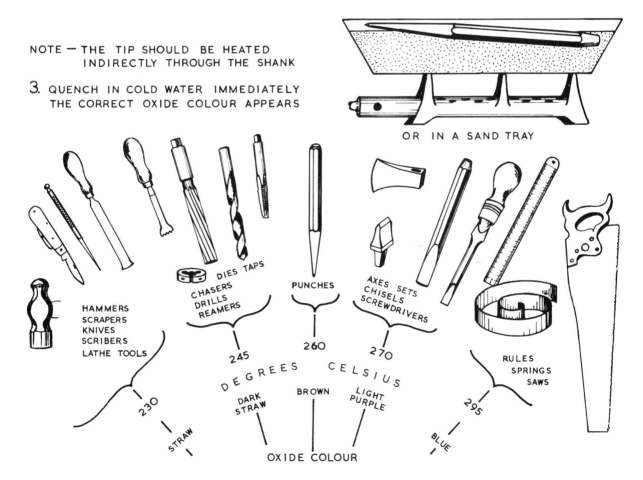

HAMMERS
SCRAPERS
KNIVES
SCRIBERS
LATHE TOOLS

DIES TAPS
CHASERS
DRILLS
REAMERS

PUNCHES

AXES SETS
CHISELS
SCREWDRIVERS

RULES
SPRINGS
SAWS

245   260   270

230   295

DEGREES CELSIUS

STRAW

DARK
STRAW

BROWN

LIGHT
PURPLE

BLUE

OXIDE COLOUR

57

HOLLOWING

Hollowing is a method of producing shallow bowl-shaped articles by beating annealed sheet metal into a hollowed wood block or a sandbag. A hammer hollows the work quicker than a mallet but in unskilled hands it will bruise and distort the work. The disc is tilted slightly and the blows are struck a very short distance from the point of support so as to push the metal a little at a time into the hollow. Constant beating will work-harden the metal and it must be softened periodically. The process is known as 'annealing'. This is done by bringing the work to a uniform dull red heat. The metal should be allowed to cool in air. It should then be placed in an acid solution, see page 42. This dissolves the oxides formed during heating. Brass tongs should be used in the acid bath as steel tools will contaminate the acid solution. On removal from the acid the work should be thoroughly washed in running water.

Sinking is a process where the centre portion of a disc is set down as in a plate or dish, leaving a more or less flat rim round the circumference.

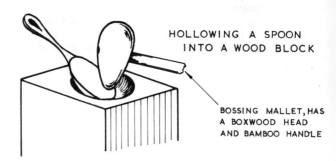

ESTIMATING THE SIZE OF BLANK REQUIRED

2 x A = DIA. OF BLANK

2 x A + B = DIA. OF BLANK

THE METAL STRETCHES DURING HAMMERING, THUS MAKING UP THE DIFFERENCE IN MEASUREMENT BETWEEN THE CHORD AND THE ARC

HOLLOWING A SPOON INTO A WOOD BLOCK

BOSSING MALLET, HAS A BOXWOOD HEAD AND BAMBOO HANDLE

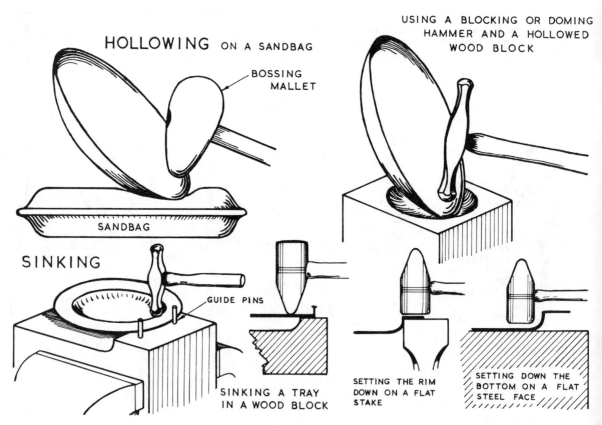

HOLLOWING ON A SANDBAG

BOSSING MALLET

SANDBAG

USING A BLOCKING OR DOMING HAMMER AND A HOLLOWED WOOD BLOCK

SINKING

SINKING A TRAY IN A WOOD BLOCK

GUIDE PINS

SETTING THE RIM DOWN ON A FLAT STAKE

SETTING DOWN THE BOTTOM ON A FLAT STEEL FACE

RAISING

Raising is a method of producing deep bowls and hollow-ware. These are often given a preliminary hollowing as shown on page 58 and then are raised to the final size and shape. In raising, the disc is beaten from the outside while supported on a suitable stake. The work is tilted slightly and the blows are struck a little forward of the point of support so that the metal is pushed down on to the stake. The blows should not be so heavy that they thin out the metal. A ring of blows is struck round the work leaving a definite ridge. This ridge is carried up the work by further courses of raising, working in concentric circles from the base to the rim. As the raising proceeds the diameter of the work decreases and at the same time the height of the work increases. Frequent annealing and pickling are required as the metal becomes work-hardened.

RAISING A VASE

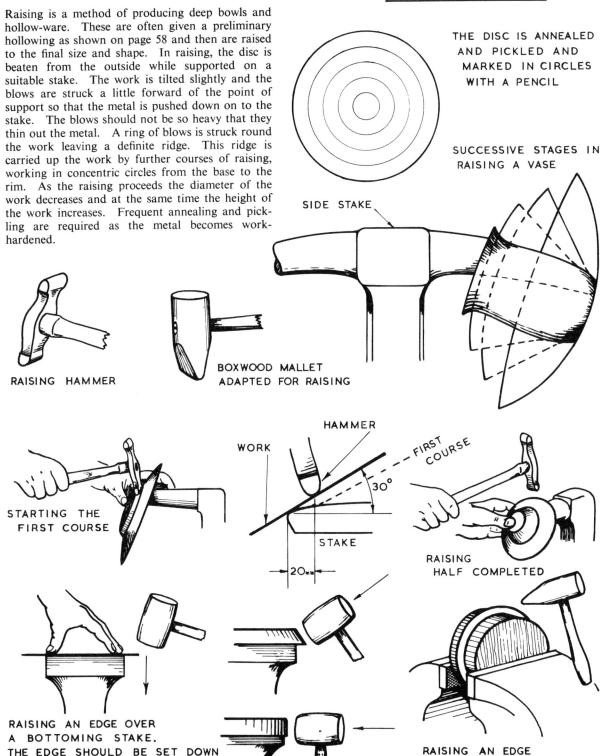

THE DISC IS ANNEALED AND PICKLED AND MARKED IN CIRCLES WITH A PENCIL

SUCCESSIVE STAGES IN RAISING A VASE

SIDE STAKE

RAISING HAMMER

BOXWOOD MALLET ADAPTED FOR RAISING

STARTING THE FIRST COURSE

WORK

HAMMER

FIRST COURSE

30°

STAKE

20

RAISING HALF COMPLETED

RAISING AN EDGE OVER A BOTTOMING STAKE. THE EDGE SHOULD BE SET DOWN GRADUALLY IN SUCCESSIVE COURSES

RAISING AN EDGE BETWEEN WOOD DISCS

59

PLANISHING

Planishing is a process which removes blemishes left by previous tool usage; it enables the work to be accurately finished to size and contour, and work-hardens the metal, thus imparting strength to the finished article. The facets left on the work by the planishing hammer may be left in as a form of surface decoration or they can be polished out. When the work has been brought to the finished size and shape it is annealed, pickled, scoured with pumice powder, washed and dried. A stake, or a series of stakes, is selected to fit the profile of the work. The work is then trapped between a stake and the slightly domed face of the planishing hammer by a light yet firm blow. This light hammering proceeds in concentric circles, usually working out from the centre, until the whole surface of the work has been planished. The hammer face and the stake should be highly polished in order to impart a smooth finish to the surface of the work.

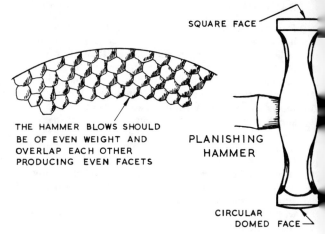

SQUARE FACE

THE HAMMER BLOWS SHOULD BE OF EVEN WEIGHT AND OVERLAP EACH OTHER PRODUCING EVEN FACETS

PLANISHING HAMMER

CIRCULAR DOMED FACE

PLANISHING A BOWL

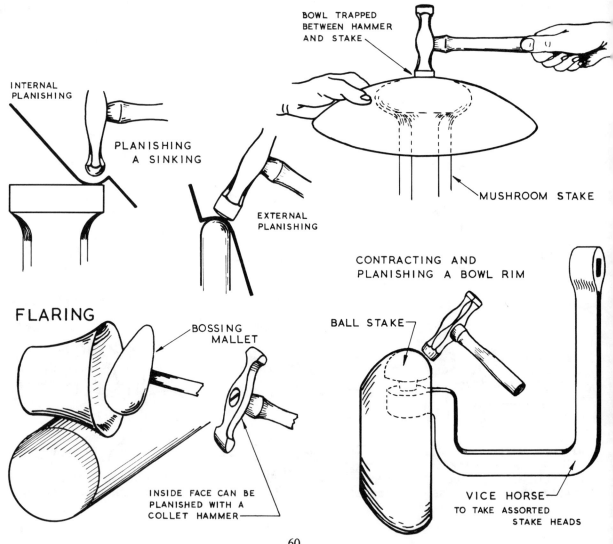

BOWL TRAPPED BETWEEN HAMMER AND STAKE

MUSHROOM STAKE

INTERNAL PLANISHING

PLANISHING A SINKING

EXTERNAL PLANISHING

CONTRACTING AND PLANISHING A BOWL RIM

BALL STAKE

VICE HORSE
TO TAKE ASSORTED STAKE HEADS

FLARING

BOSSING MALLET

INSIDE FACE CAN BE PLANISHED WITH A COLLET HAMMER

CASTING

Castings are made by pouring molten metal into a mould and allowing it to solidify. Materials having low melting points, such as plastics and zinc alloys, are usually cast in steel moulds or dies. These can be used to produce thousands of castings before they erode sufficiently to require renewing. This process is termed 'die casting'. When the liquid metal is forced into a mould by a ram it is termed 'pressure die casting'. All heavy work and metals with high melting points are traditionally cast in moulding sand. A modern development is the preparation of moulds from a mixture of moulding sand and powdered plastic. This is useful for large intricate castings where the mould can be made in several pieces, all of which are baked to harden them, and then assembled and clamped together with long bolts obviating the use of a moulding flask.

Moulding sands all have high melting points, contain sufficient clay to bind the grains together yet are permeable to allow the escape of gases. The minimum amount of water is added to the sand to enable it just to cling when squeezed. Too much water will generate steam, blowing the mould open when the hot metal is poured. Too dry a mix will not hold the shape of the pattern.

THE CUPOLA FURNACE The Cupola does not work continuously but is re-lighted for each melt. Once the bed coke is burning, pig and scrap iron, limestone and more coke are added and the air blast turned on. The molten metal runs down into the base and is tapped off for pouring into prepared moulds.

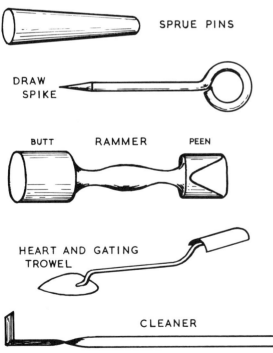

SPRUE PINS

DRAW SPIKE

BUTT   RAMMER   PEEN

HEART AND GATING TROWEL

CLEANER

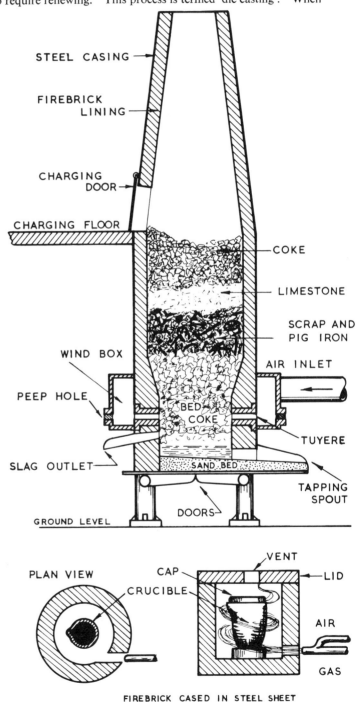

STEEL CASING

FIREBRICK LINING

CHARGING DOOR

CHARGING FLOOR

COKE

LIMESTONE

SCRAP AND PIG IRON

AIR INLET

WIND BOX

PEEP HOLE

BED COKE

TUYERE

SLAG OUTLET

SAND BED

TAPPING SPOUT

GROUND LEVEL   DOORS

VENT

PLAN VIEW   CAP   LID

CRUCIBLE

AIR

GAS

FIREBRICK CASED IN STEEL SHEET

PATTERNS

The pattern is a copy of the finished article. It is usually made from wood and is larger than the finished work in order to allow for shrinkage in the metal while cooling from the liquid to the solid state.

The pattern is placed on a turn over board, the drag inverted over it. The whole is then dusted with parting powder (burnt clay or French chalk) and covered with a 20 mm layer of facing sand. This is new sand passed through a fine sieve and mixed with a small amount of Fuller's earth, loam and coal dust. Old sand is then added and rammed down. More sand is added and rammed until the drag is full. The top is strickled off, a turn over board positioned and the whole inverted. Loose sand is blown away from the sand pattern and the sand face. The whole is dusted with parting powder, the cope fitted and sprue pins inserted.

The runner should be close to the bulkiest part of the pattern and the riser placed on the opposite side. The cope is then rammed full and strickled in a similar manner to the drag. The sprue pins are removed and the top of the holes rounded to a funnel shape. The flask is then opened and channels are cut linking the pattern to the runner and riser. Vent holes are pricked to allow dispersal of gases, particularly in any places where they may be trapped. The pattern is then removed with the draw spike and loose sand blown clear. Any necessary cores are then placed in position. Cores are made from clay-free sand mixed with raw linseed oil as a binder. This mixture is pressed into shape in a core box and baked hard in an oven. The mould is then closed and the two halves locked together to prevent molten metal from flushing out through the joint.

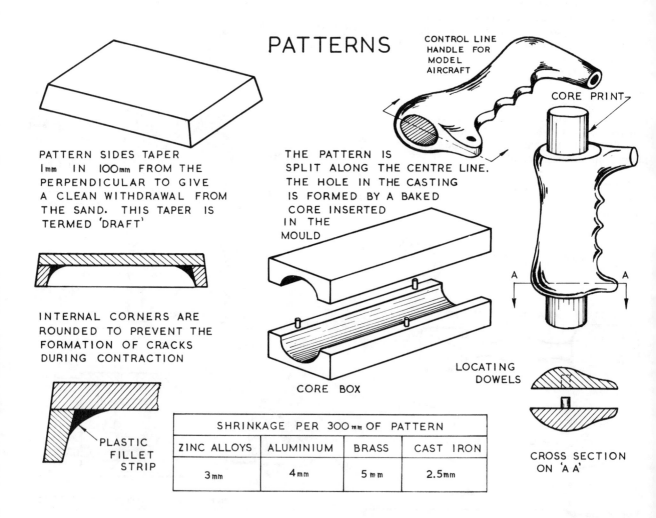

PATTERNS

PATTERN SIDES TAPER
1mm IN 100mm FROM THE
PERPENDICULAR TO GIVE
A CLEAN WITHDRAWAL FROM
THE SAND. THIS TAPER IS
TERMED 'DRAFT'

INTERNAL CORNERS ARE
ROUNDED TO PREVENT THE
FORMATION OF CRACKS
DURING CONTRACTION

PLASTIC
FILLET
STRIP

THE PATTERN IS
SPLIT ALONG THE CENTRE LINE.
THE HOLE IN THE CASTING
IS FORMED BY A BAKED
CORE INSERTED
IN THE
MOULD

CORE BOX

LOCATING
DOWELS

CONTROL LINE
HANDLE FOR
MODEL
AIRCRAFT

CORE PRINT

CROSS SECTION
ON 'A A'

SHRINKAGE PER 300 mm OF PATTERN			
ZINC ALLOYS	ALUMINIUM	BRASS	CAST IRON
3 mm	4 mm	5 mm	2.5mm

PREPARING A MOULD

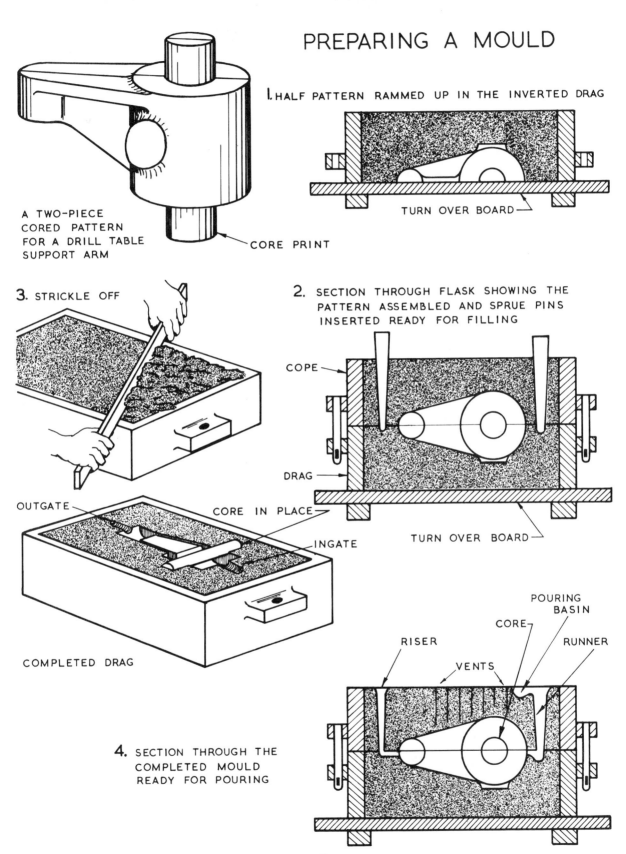

A TWO-PIECE CORED PATTERN FOR A DRILL TABLE SUPPORT ARM

CORE PRINT

1. HALF PATTERN RAMMED UP IN THE INVERTED DRAG

TURN OVER BOARD

3. STRICKLE OFF

OUTGATE

CORE IN PLACE

INGATE

COMPLETED DRAG

2. SECTION THROUGH FLASK SHOWING THE PATTERN ASSEMBLED AND SPRUE PINS INSERTED READY FOR FILLING

COPE

DRAG

TURN OVER BOARD

POURING BASIN

CORE

RISER

RUNNER

VENTS

4. SECTION THROUGH THE COMPLETED MOULD READY FOR POURING

DRILLING

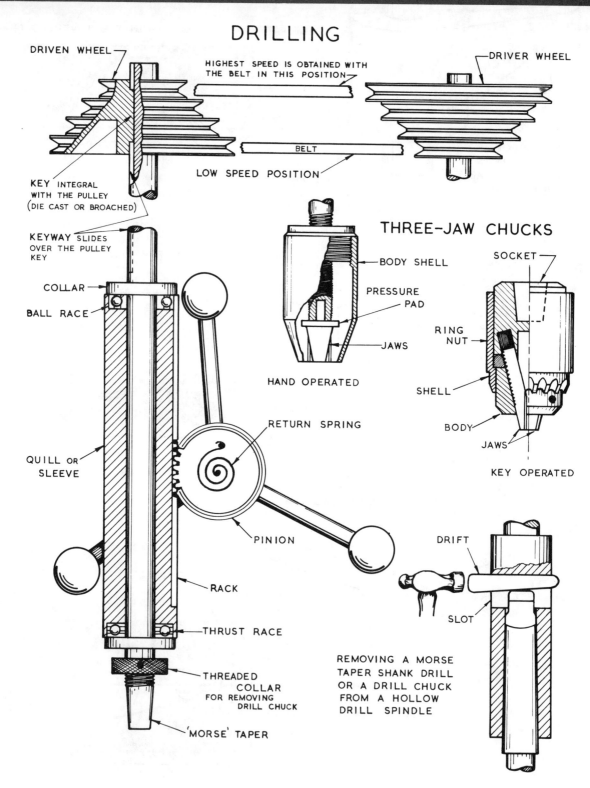

DRIVEN WHEEL

HIGHEST SPEED IS OBTAINED WITH
THE BELT IN THIS POSITION

DRIVER WHEEL

BELT

LOW SPEED POSITION

KEY INTEGRAL
WITH THE PULLEY
(DIE CAST OR BROACHED)

KEYWAY SLIDES
OVER THE PULLEY
KEY

COLLAR

BALL RACE

QUILL OR
SLEEVE

RACK

THRUST RACE

THREADED
COLLAR
FOR REMOVING
DRILL CHUCK

'MORSE' TAPER

RETURN SPRING

PINION

THREE-JAW CHUCKS

BODY SHELL

PRESSURE
PAD

JAWS

HAND OPERATED

SOCKET

RING
NUT

SHELL

BODY

JAWS

KEY OPERATED

DRIFT

SLOT

REMOVING A MORSE
TAPER SHANK DRILL
OR A DRILL CHUCK
FROM A HOLLOW
DRILL SPINDLE

TWIST DRILLS

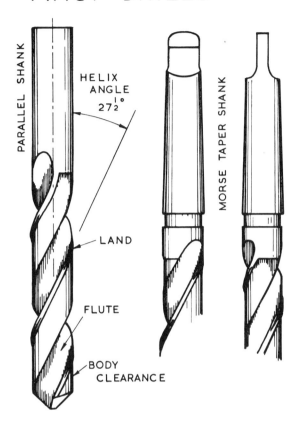

PARALLEL SHANK

HELIX ANGLE 27½°

MORSE TAPER SHANK

LAND

FLUTE

BODY CLEARANCE

Twist drills are made either from carbon steel, hardened and tempered, or from high speed steel. Carbon drills are used for slow running, mainly in hand braces. High speed steel drills are for use in power-driven machines. Flat or spade bits can be made in the workshop from silver steel rod but they are inaccurate for deep holes.

Good Drilling Practice

When drilling large holes it is customary to drill a small pilot hole first.

Small drills are always started in centre punch dots.

Make sure the drill is sharp; if in doubt re-grind.

Clamp the drill securely in the chuck.

Make sure the drill runs true.

Securely clamp the work.

Set the correct speed and feed.

Use a suitable cutting oil.

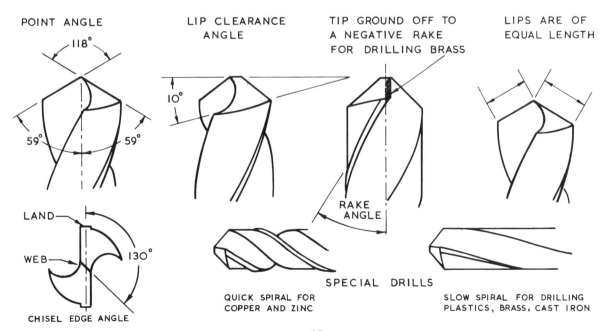

POINT ANGLE

118°

59° 59°

LAND

WEB

130°

CHISEL EDGE ANGLE

LIP CLEARANCE ANGLE

10°

TIP GROUND OFF TO A NEGATIVE RAKE FOR DRILLING BRASS

RAKE ANGLE

LIPS ARE OF EQUAL LENGTH

SPECIAL DRILLS

QUICK SPIRAL FOR COPPER AND ZINC

SLOW SPIRAL FOR DRILLING PLASTICS, BRASS, CAST IRON

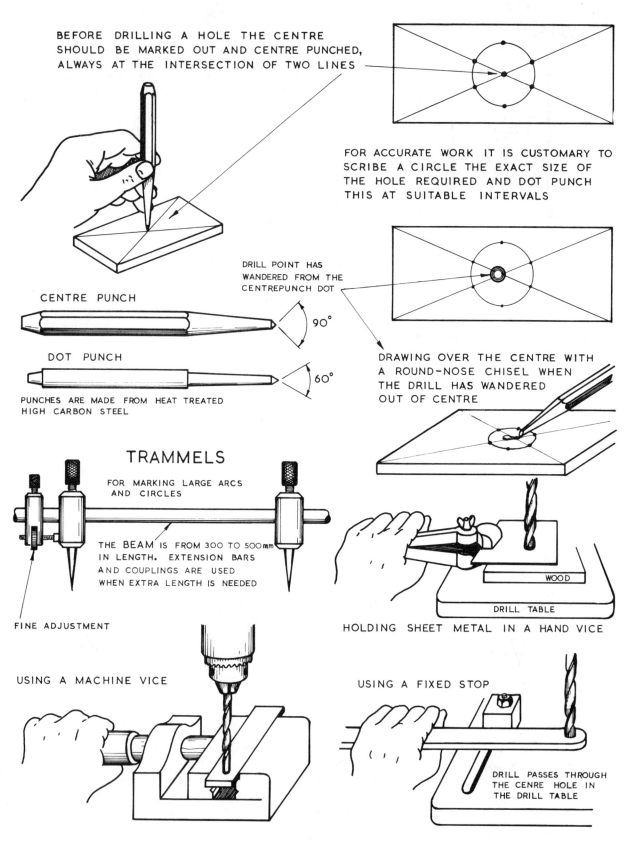

BEFORE DRILLING A HOLE THE CENTRE SHOULD BE MARKED OUT AND CENTRE PUNCHED, ALWAYS AT THE INTERSECTION OF TWO LINES

FOR ACCURATE WORK IT IS CUSTOMARY TO SCRIBE A CIRCLE THE EXACT SIZE OF THE HOLE REQUIRED AND DOT PUNCH THIS AT SUITABLE INTERVALS

CENTRE PUNCH

90°

DRILL POINT HAS WANDERED FROM THE CENTREPUNCH DOT

DOT PUNCH

60°

PUNCHES ARE MADE FROM HEAT TREATED HIGH CARBON STEEL

DRAWING OVER THE CENTRE WITH A ROUND-NOSE CHISEL WHEN THE DRILL HAS WANDERED OUT OF CENTRE

TRAMMELS

FOR MARKING LARGE ARCS AND CIRCLES

THE BEAM IS FROM 300 TO 500 mm IN LENGTH. EXTENSION BARS AND COUPLINGS ARE USED WHEN EXTRA LENGTH IS NEEDED

FINE ADJUSTMENT

WOOD

DRILL TABLE

HOLDING SHEET METAL IN A HAND VICE

USING A MACHINE VICE

USING A FIXED STOP

DRILL PASSES THROUGH THE CENRE HOLE IN THE DRILL TABLE

DIAMOND POINT OR SPADE DRILL

THESE CAN BE MADE FROM SILVER STEEL
ROD, FORGED OUT, HARDENED AND TEMPERED

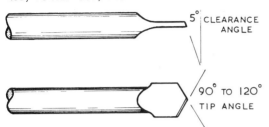

5° CLEARANCE
ANGLE

90° TO 120°
TIP ANGLE

COUNTERSINK

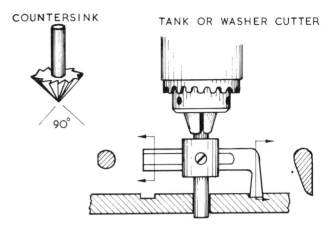

90°

TANK OR WASHER CUTTER

THE CENTRE HOLE IS DRILLED FIRST.
THE CUTTER BAR IS ADJUSTABLE FOR
DIFFERENT DIAMETERS

STRAIGHT FLUTED DRILL

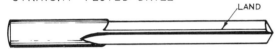

LAND

THE STRAIGHT FLUTES GIVE NO RAKE TO THE
CUTTING EDGES, RESULTING IN A SCRAPING
ACTION SPECIALLY SUITED TO CUTTING BRASS

PIN DRILL OR SPOT FACER DRILL

HSS

SPOT FACER MADE FROM
A SILVER STEEL ROD AND A
HARDENED CARBON STEEL
BUSH

COMBINATION DRILL AND COUNTERSINK

HSS

ALSO TERMED 'SLOCOMBE' OR 'CENTRE DRILL'
FOR CENTRING BARS IN THE LATHE

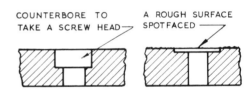

COUNTERBORE TO
TAKE A SCREW HEAD

A ROUGH SURFACE
SPOTFACED

'D' BIT FOR TRUING A DRILLED HOLE AND PRODUCING A FLAT BOTTOM

5° CLEARANCE

MADE FROM HARDENED AND TEMPERED SILVER STEEL

MORSE TAPER SLEEVE

TO HOLD A SMALL TAPER SHANK DRILL
IN A LARGER TAPERED HOLE

REAMERS USED FOR ACCURATELY FINISHING EXISTING HOLES

SPIRAL FLUTE PARALLEL REAMER

HSS

CROSS SECTION THROUGH REAMER FLUTES

TAPER REAMER OR BROACH FOR TAPER PINS

PENTAGONAL
CROSS SECTION

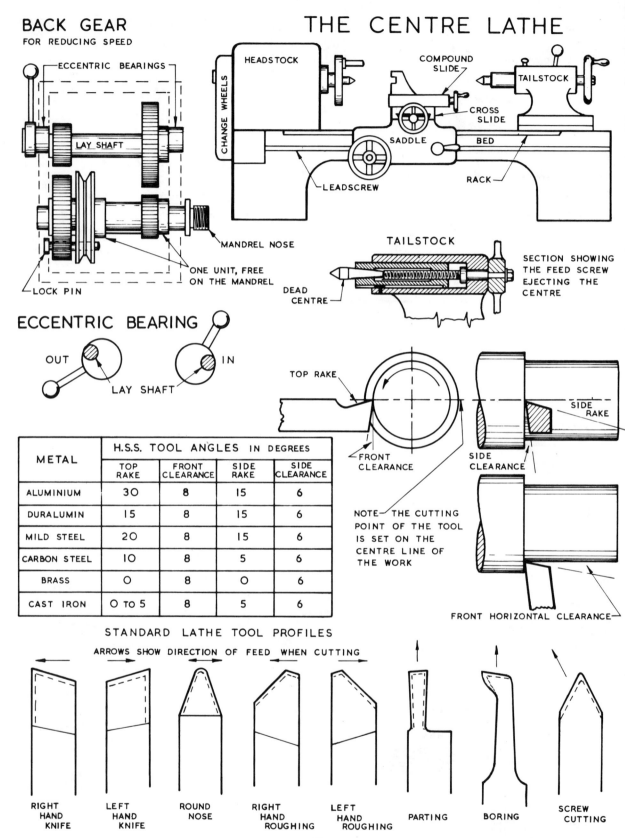

BACK GEAR
FOR REDUCING SPEED

ECCENTRIC BEARINGS

LAY SHAFT

MANDREL NOSE

ONE UNIT, FREE ON THE MANDREL

LOCK PIN

ECCENTRIC BEARING

OUT IN

LAY SHAFT

THE CENTRE LATHE

HEADSTOCK

COMPOUND SLIDE

TAILSTOCK

CHANGE WHEELS

CROSS SLIDE

SADDLE BED

LEADSCREW

RACK

TAILSTOCK

SECTION SHOWING THE FEED SCREW EJECTING THE CENTRE

DEAD CENTRE

TOP RAKE

SIDE RAKE

FRONT CLEARANCE

SIDE CLEARANCE

NOTE—THE CUTTING POINT OF THE TOOL IS SET ON THE CENTRE LINE OF THE WORK

FRONT HORIZONTAL CLEARANCE

METAL	H.S.S. TOOL ANGLES IN DEGREES			
	TOP RAKE	FRONT CLEARANCE	SIDE RAKE	SIDE CLEARANCE
ALUMINIUM	30	8	15	6
DURALUMIN	15	8	15	6
MILD STEEL	20	8	15	6
CARBON STEEL	10	8	5	6
BRASS	O	8	O	6
CAST IRON	O TO 5	8	5	6

STANDARD LATHE TOOL PROFILES

ARROWS SHOW DIRECTION OF FEED WHEN CUTTING

RIGHT HAND KNIFE

LEFT HAND KNIFE

ROUND NOSE

RIGHT HAND ROUGHING

LEFT HAND ROUGHING

PARTING

BORING

SCREW CUTTING

FACING (SURFACING)

1. SETTING UP

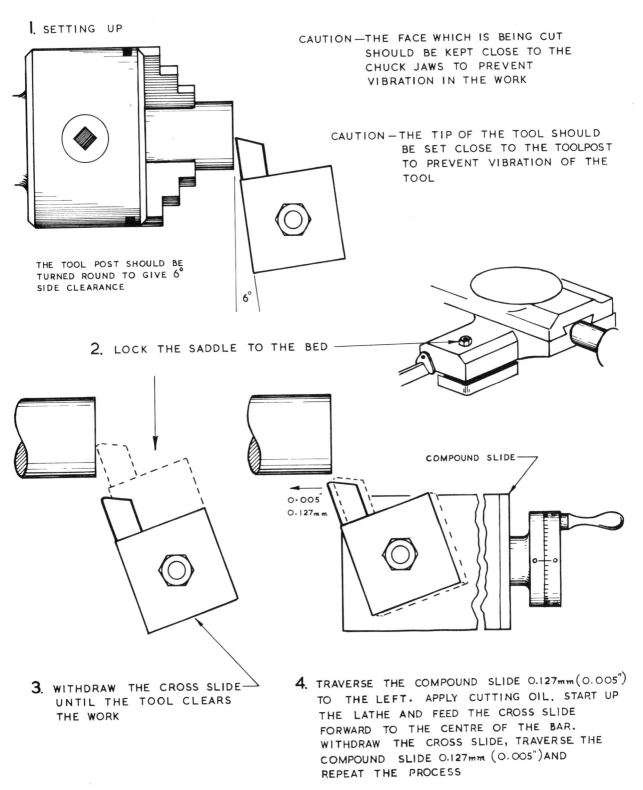

CAUTION—THE FACE WHICH IS BEING CUT SHOULD BE KEPT CLOSE TO THE CHUCK JAWS TO PREVENT VIBRATION IN THE WORK

CAUTION—THE TIP OF THE TOOL SHOULD BE SET CLOSE TO THE TOOLPOST TO PREVENT VIBRATION OF THE TOOL

THE TOOL POST SHOULD BE TURNED ROUND TO GIVE 6° SIDE CLEARANCE

6°

2. LOCK THE SADDLE TO THE BED

COMPOUND SLIDE

0·005"
0·127mm

3. WITHDRAW THE CROSS SLIDE UNTIL THE TOOL CLEARS THE WORK

4. TRAVERSE THE COMPOUND SLIDE 0.127mm (0.005") TO THE LEFT. APPLY CUTTING OIL. START UP THE LATHE AND FEED THE CROSS SLIDE FORWARD TO THE CENTRE OF THE BAR. WITHDRAW THE CROSS SLIDE, TRAVERSE THE COMPOUND SLIDE 0.127mm (0.005") AND REPEAT THE PROCESS

PARALLEL TURNING SHORT WORK (TRAVERSING OR SLIDING)

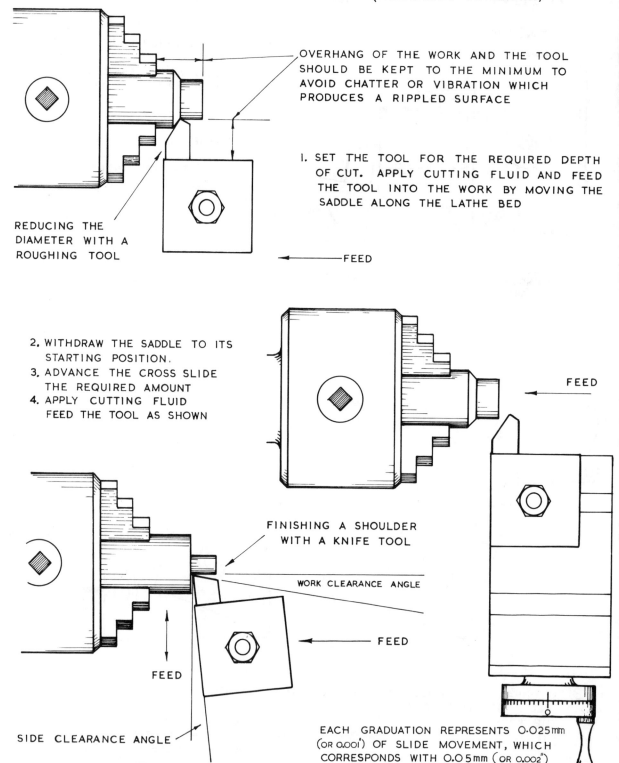

OVERHANG OF THE WORK AND THE TOOL SHOULD BE KEPT TO THE MINIMUM TO AVOID CHATTER OR VIBRATION WHICH PRODUCES A RIPPLED SURFACE

1. SET THE TOOL FOR THE REQUIRED DEPTH OF CUT. APPLY CUTTING FLUID AND FEED THE TOOL INTO THE WORK BY MOVING THE SADDLE ALONG THE LATHE BED

REDUCING THE DIAMETER WITH A ROUGHING TOOL

FEED

2. WITHDRAW THE SADDLE TO ITS STARTING POSITION.
3. ADVANCE THE CROSS SLIDE THE REQUIRED AMOUNT
4. APPLY CUTTING FLUID FEED THE TOOL AS SHOWN

FEED

FINISHING A SHOULDER WITH A KNIFE TOOL

WORK CLEARANCE ANGLE

FEED

FEED

SIDE CLEARANCE ANGLE

EACH GRADUATION REPRESENTS 0.025mm (OR 0.001") OF SLIDE MOVEMENT, WHICH CORRESPONDS WITH 0.05mm (OR 0.002") OF WORK DIAMETER

70

PARALLEL TURNING LONG WORK

LONG WORK SHOULD BE FACED AND
AND CENTRE DRILLED AT ONE END

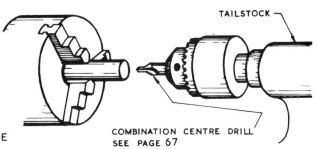

TAILSTOCK

COMBINATION CENTRE DRILL
SEE PAGE 67

AND THEN SUPPORTED AT THE OUTER
END BY MEANS OF A TAILSTOCK CENTRE

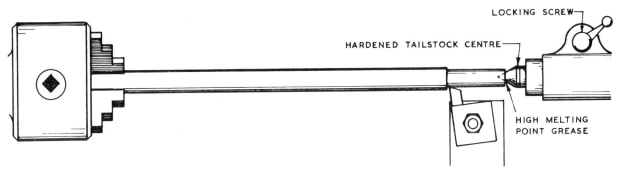

LOCKING SCREW

HARDENED TAILSTOCK CENTRE

HIGH MELTING
POINT GREASE

TO PREVENT THE WORK VIBRATING IN THE MIDDLE A TWO-POINT
TRAVELLING STEADY IS MOUNTED ON THE CROSS SLIDE. THIS
TAKES THE THRUST OF THE CUTTING TOOL

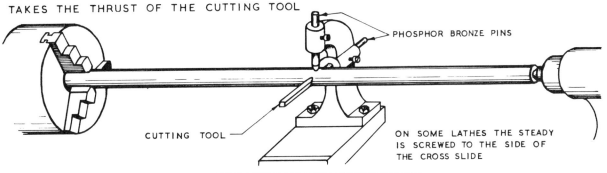

PHOSPHOR BRONZE PINS

CUTTING TOOL

ON SOME LATHES THE STEADY
IS SCREWED TO THE SIDE OF
THE CROSS SLIDE

METALS	CUTTING SPEED PER MINUTE			
	ROUGHING 0.5 mm (0.02")		FINISHING 0.15 mm (0.006")	
	METRES	FEET	METRES	FEET
GREY CAST IRON	15	50	22·5	75
CARBON STEEL	12	40	18	60
MILD STEEL	24	80	45	150
BRASS	60	200	105	350
ALUMINIUM ALLOY	90	300	180	600
SOFT ALUMINIUM	105	350	225	750

SPINDLE SPEED
IN REVOLUTIONS PER
MINUTE =

$$\frac{\text{CUTTING SPEED} \times 1000}{\pi \times \text{DIA IN mm}}$$

$$\frac{\text{CUTTING SPEED} \times 12}{\pi \times \text{DIA IN INCHES}}$$

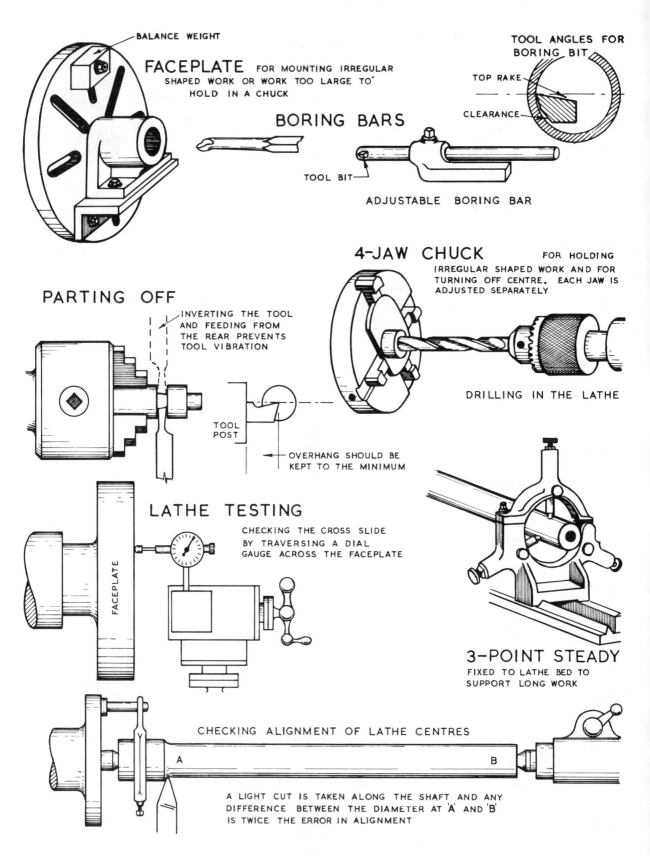

BALANCE WEIGHT

FACEPLATE FOR MOUNTING IRREGULAR SHAPED WORK OR WORK TOO LARGE TO HOLD IN A CHUCK

TOOL ANGLES FOR BORING BIT

TOP RAKE

CLEARANCE

BORING BARS

TOOL BIT

ADJUSTABLE BORING BAR

4-JAW CHUCK FOR HOLDING IRREGULAR SHAPED WORK AND FOR TURNING OFF CENTRE. EACH JAW IS ADJUSTED SEPARATELY

PARTING OFF

INVERTING THE TOOL AND FEEDING FROM THE REAR PREVENTS TOOL VIBRATION

TOOL POST

OVERHANG SHOULD BE KEPT TO THE MINIMUM

DRILLING IN THE LATHE

LATHE TESTING

CHECKING THE CROSS SLIDE BY TRAVERSING A DIAL GAUGE ACROSS THE FACEPLATE

FACEPLATE

3-POINT STEADY
FIXED TO LATHE BED TO SUPPORT LONG WORK

CHECKING ALIGNMENT OF LATHE CENTRES

A   B

A LIGHT CUT IS TAKEN ALONG THE SHAFT AND ANY DIFFERENCE BETWEEN THE DIAMETER AT 'A' AND 'B' IS TWICE THE ERROR IN ALIGNMENT

TURNING BETWEEN CENTRES

Internal wear in the three-jaw chuck scroll leads to lack of concentricity if it should be necessary to remove and later replace work in the chuck. Therefore, when work has to be changed end for end, or removed and replaced, it is customary to mount it between centres for turning.

The work should be centre drilled and faced across each end. Long work will need a travelling steady, as on page 71. The hardened centre fits in the tailstock and the soft centre in the tapered sleeve, which in turn fits in the headstock mandrel. The catchplate screws on to the mandrel nose. The mating surfaces of all these should be thoroughly cleaned when assembling. The tailstock centre should be greased and adjusted so that the work spins freely yet without end play. This should be checked again while turning as the work expands through frictional heating and may bind between the centres. The tailstock and its barrel should both be secured with the appropriate locking screws before turning commences. The feed should be towards the headstock so that the pressure of the cut is taken by the revolving centre.

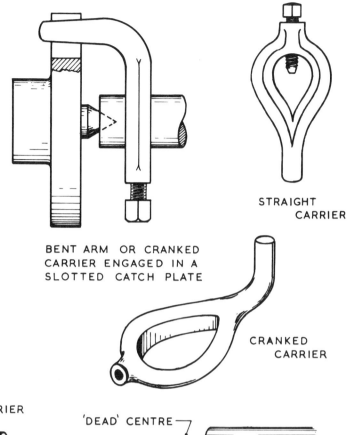

STRAIGHT CARRIER

BENT ARM OR CRANKED CARRIER ENGAGED IN A SLOTTED CATCH PLATE

CRANKED CARRIER

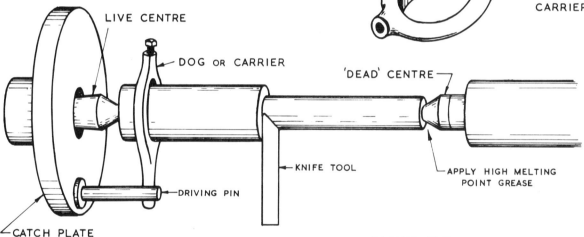

LIVE CENTRE

DOG OR CARRIER

'DEAD' CENTRE

KNIFE TOOL

APPLY HIGH MELTING POINT GREASE

DRIVING PIN

CATCH PLATE

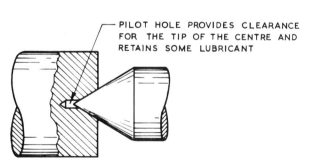

PILOT HOLE PROVIDES CLEARANCE FOR THE TIP OF THE CENTRE AND RETAINS SOME LUBRICANT

THE MATCHING TAPERS OF THE CENTRE AND THE HOLE PROVIDE A CONICAL BEARING SURFACE

FACING THE BAR END

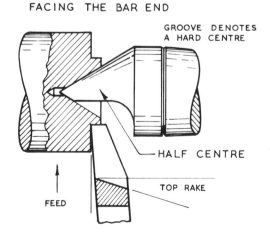

GROOVE DENOTES A HARD CENTRE

HALF CENTRE

TOP RAKE

FEED

TURNING SHORT TAPERS

Either the base of the compound slide or the top face of the cross slide is in the form of a circular plate which is marked off in degrees. The opposite plate carries a zero mark. When this zero mark coincides with the O° mark, the compound slide is parallel with the lathe bed. For turning short tapers, either internal or external, the compound slide may be set over to any desired angle by loosening the locking screws in its base. When the slide is set to the required angle the screws are tightened up again to lock it in position. The tool should be set with its cutting point exactly level with the tip of the lathe centre (centre height). The saddle should be locked to the bed of the lathe and the tool traversed across the work by means of the hand feed on the compound slide.

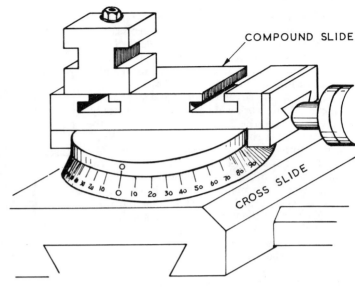

COMPOUND SLIDE

CROSS SLIDE

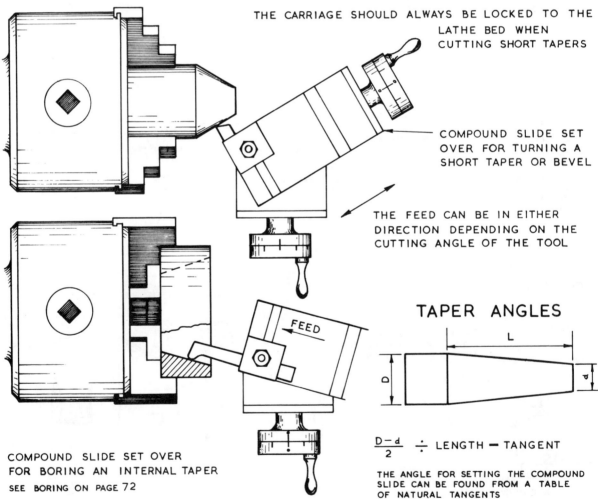

THE CARRIAGE SHOULD ALWAYS BE LOCKED TO THE LATHE BED WHEN CUTTING SHORT TAPERS

COMPOUND SLIDE SET OVER FOR TURNING A SHORT TAPER OR BEVEL

THE FEED CAN BE IN EITHER DIRECTION DEPENDING ON THE CUTTING ANGLE OF THE TOOL

FEED

COMPOUND SLIDE SET OVER FOR BORING AN INTERNAL TAPER

SEE BORING ON PAGE 72

TAPER ANGLES

$$\frac{D-d}{2} \div \text{LENGTH} = \text{TANGENT}$$

THE ANGLE FOR SETTING THE COMPOUND SLIDE CAN BE FOUND FROM A TABLE OF NATURAL TANGENTS

TURNING LONG TAPERS

It is customary to machine long tapers by off-setting the tailstock. The amount of off-set is calculated as follows:

Amount of off-set =

$$\frac{\text{Length of work in mm}}{1000} \times \frac{\text{Taper per metre}}{2}$$

$$\frac{(\text{Length of work in inches}}{12} \times \frac{\text{Taper per foot})}{2}$$

The tailstock can be moved over a small amount only before the centres bind in the centre-drilled holes in the ends of the work, as shown at the foot of the page. Two methods of overcoming this fault are shown. If the taper exceeds two or three degrees it is better to use a special taper turning attachment. In the one illustrated the cross slide is freed from its drive nut and is linked to a slider block on an adjustable slide. The work is then mounted between centres in the normal manner and the saddle traversed along the bed, when the cross slide will follow the angle set on the adjustable slide.

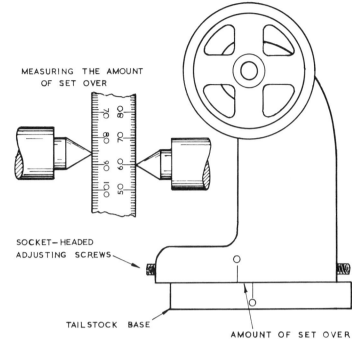

MEASURING THE AMOUNT OF SET OVER

SOCKET—HEADED ADJUSTING SCREWS

TAILSTOCK BASE

AMOUNT OF SET OVER

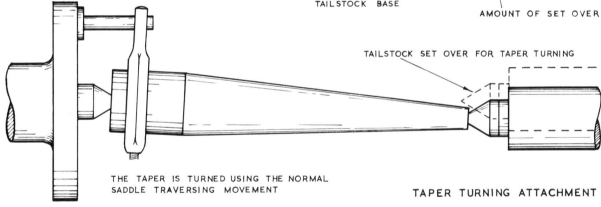

TAILSTOCK SET OVER FOR TAPER TURNING

THE TAPER IS TURNED USING THE NORMAL SADDLE TRAVERSING MOVEMENT

TAPER TURNING ATTACHMENT

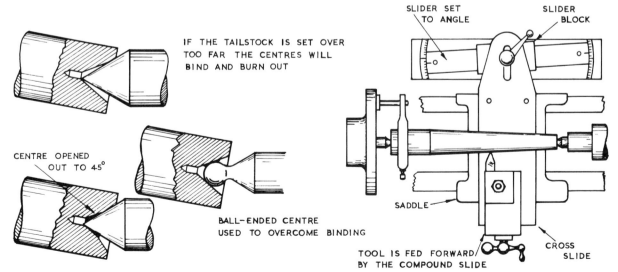

IF THE TAILSTOCK IS SET OVER TOO FAR THE CENTRES WILL BIND AND BURN OUT

CENTRE OPENED OUT TO 45°

BALL—ENDED CENTRE USED TO OVERCOME BINDING

SLIDER SET TO ANGLE

SLIDER BLOCK

SADDLE

CROSS SLIDE

TOOL IS FED FORWARD BY THE COMPOUND SLIDE

SCREWCUTTING

The cutting of screw threads in the lathe is carried out by traversing the cutting tool at a definite rate in proportion to the rate at which the work revolves. Movement is imparted to the tool through the saddle, which is traversed by the movement of the leadscrew nut along the leadscrew. This latter is driven by gearing from the mandrel. Thus, if the driving wheel on the mandrel is the same size as the driven wheel on the leadscrew (and there is only one intermediate wheel between the two), the lead screw and the mandrel will both revolve at the same speed and the pitch of the screw being cut will be the same as the pitch of the leadscrew. If the driven wheel is twice the size of the driver wheel it will revolve at half the speed, as will the leadscrew; therefore the finished work will have twice the number of threads as the leadscrew, i.e. a finer thread.

The sizes of gear wheels required to produce threads of any given pitch are usually specified in a list which is fastened to the inside of the change wheel guard. Alternatively, they can be found by using the ratio:

Metric Lead Screws

$$\frac{\text{Pitch to be cut}}{\text{Pitch of leadscrew}} = \frac{1 \text{ mm}}{3 \text{ mm}} = \frac{1}{3} = \frac{\text{Driver gear wheel}}{\text{Driven gear wheel}}$$

But there are no gears with so few teeth, so we use a common multiplier:

$$\frac{1 \times 40}{3 \times 40} = \frac{40}{120} = \frac{\text{Driver gear}}{\text{Driven gear}}$$

Motion is transmitted between the 40 teeth and the 120 teeth wheels by an intermediate wheel termed an 'idler' wheel. The size of the idler wheel has no effect upon the gear ratio. This cluster of three wheels is known as a 'simple train'.

English Lead Screws

$$\frac{\text{Pitch to be cut}}{\text{Pitch of leadscrew}} = \frac{1 \text{ mm}}{1 \text{ in}} = \frac{1 \text{ mm}}{25.4 \text{ mm}} = \text{ratio} \frac{1}{25.4} = \frac{5}{127}$$

Thus a 127 teeth gear is needed for cutting metric threads from an English leadscrew:

$$\frac{\text{Pitch to be cut}}{\text{Pitch of leadscrew}} = \frac{4 \text{ mm}}{8 \text{ t.p.i.}} = \frac{5 \times 4 \times 8}{127} = \frac{160 \text{ Driver}}{127 \text{ Driven}}$$

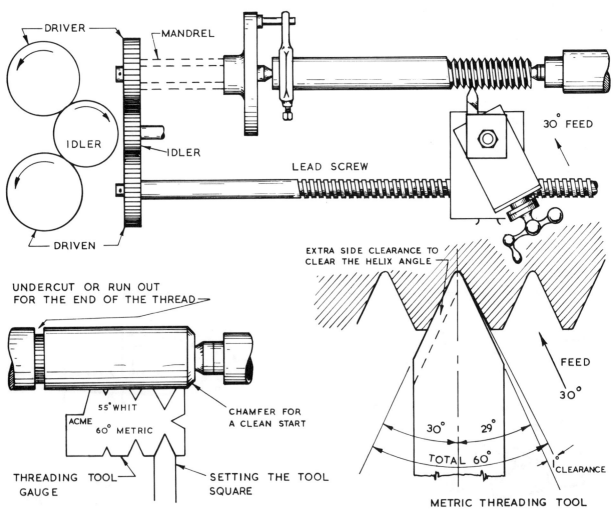

DRIVER — MANDREL — IDLER — IDLER — DRIVEN — LEAD SCREW — 30° FEED

UNDERCUT OR RUN OUT FOR THE END OF THE THREAD

CHAMFER FOR A CLEAN START

55° WHIT — ACME — 60° METRIC

THREADING TOOL GAUGE — SETTING THE TOOL SQUARE

EXTRA SIDE CLEARANCE TO CLEAR THE HELIX ANGLE

FEED 30°

30° · 29°

TOTAL 60°

1° CLEARANCE

METRIC THREADING TOOL

Provision is made on some lathes to run a pair of 44 and 52 teeth gears in combination with a 30 teeth wheel, as 44 x 30 ÷ 52 = 25.4, the metric equivalent of 1 inch. If it is required to cut a thread where the necessary gear wheels are outside the normal range, then a 'compound train' is used. The pitch to be cut is set over the pitch of the leadscrew as before and then the resulting fraction is suitably divided to give two fractions:

$$\frac{\text{Pitch to be cut}}{\text{Pitch of leadscrew}} = \frac{0.9 \text{ mm}}{3 \text{ mm}} = \frac{9}{30} = \frac{3 \times 3}{5 \times 6}$$

These small numbers are multiplied as in the simple train to give numbers of teeth within the available range:

$$\frac{3}{5} \times 10 = \frac{30}{50} \text{ and } \frac{3}{6} \times 10 = \frac{30}{60} = \frac{\text{Driver}}{\text{Driven}}$$

The resultant train is shown below.

When the change wheels have been assembled and the cutting tool set, the leadscrew nut is engaged and a first light traversing cut made. If the workpiece is short the saddle can be returned to the start using the motor reversing switch but if the work is long it is quicker to disengage the nut and return the saddle using the hand wheel. If the required t.p.i. is an exact multiple of the leadscrew t.p.i. the split nut can be re-engaged at any point. For other whole numbers of threads the nut can be re-engaged when the short alternate lines on the thread dial indicator (or chasing dial) are opposite the datum line, and on all other threads only when the original starting line is opposite the datum line. (Left-hand threads are cut by reversing the tumbler gears, thus reversing the direction of the leadscrew.) After the thread has been cut to the full depth, the hand turning rest is fitted and an external chaser run along the thread using only a light hand pressure. This polishes the threads and rounds off the crests.

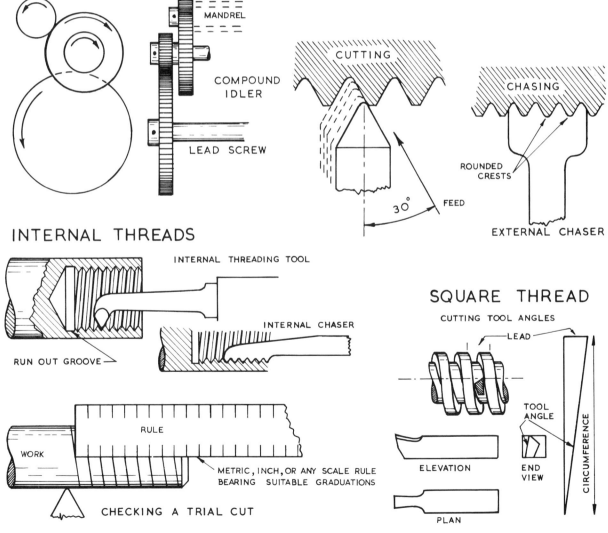

MANDREL

COMPOUND IDLER

LEAD SCREW

CUTTING

30°   FEED

CHASING

ROUNDED CRESTS

EXTERNAL CHASER

INTERNAL THREADS

INTERNAL THREADING TOOL

INTERNAL CHASER

RUN OUT GROOVE

SQUARE THREAD

CUTTING TOOL ANGLES

LEAD

TOOL ANGLE

ELEVATION   END VIEW

CIRCUMFERENCE

PLAN

RULE

WORK

METRIC, INCH, OR ANY SCALE RULE BEARING SUITABLE GRADUATIONS

CHECKING A TRIAL CUT

GRINDING

Grinding is the removal of metal by wheels made of abrasive grit. The grains form numerous tiny cutting edges which scrape small amounts of metal from the work. The ideal state in grinding is where the grains break away from the wheel as they wear smooth, thus exposing new sharp grains to continue the grinding process. This can only continue for a limited time, after which the wheel has to be dressed to a uniform surface of new sharp grains. This is done by feeding a dressing tool across the face of the wheel. The Huntington pattern is used for general grinding wheels. A diamond-tipped tool is used on fine grain wheels such as are used in precision grinding. Grinding wheels are made from the natural materials, emery and corundum, or the manufactured materials, aluminium oxide and silicon carbide. The abrasive grains are bonded by resin, silicate or rubber but more commonly by baked ceramic clays, this latter

being termed 'vitrified' bond. Wheels are designated by numbers denoting the size of the individual grains of abrasive. These sizes are measured in micrometres (a micrometre is one thousandth of a millimetre), e.g. number 8 grit measures 2415 micrometres or 2.415 mm.

Grinding wheels are clamped between dished steel flanges lined with soft thick paper washers which ensure even pressure. Old machines have holes drilled near the circumference of these flanges to permit balancing to counteract any variable density in the wheel. Modern grinding wheels are so accurately made that this is no longer necessary.

The two main functions of grinding are: off-hand grinding for sharpening small tools, carried out on a double-ended grinder as shown, and modern industrial precision grinding, where specially designed machines systematically grind components to very accurate sizes with good surface finishes.

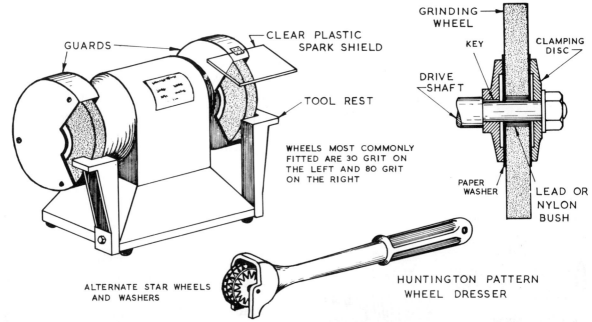

GUARDS

CLEAR PLASTIC SPARK SHIELD

TOOL REST

WHEELS MOST COMMONLY FITTED ARE 30 GRIT ON THE LEFT AND 80 GRIT ON THE RIGHT

GRINDING WHEEL

KEY

CLAMPING DISC

DRIVE SHAFT

PAPER WASHER

LEAD OR NYLON BUSH

ALTERNATE STAR WHEELS AND WASHERS

HUNTINGTON PATTERN WHEEL DRESSER

ABRASIVE		GRAIN SIZE				GRADE OF BOND			TYPE OF BOND	
		COARSE	MEDIUM	FINE	VERY FINE	SOFT	MEDIUM	HARD		
ALUMINIUM OXIDE	A	8 10 12 14	30 36 46 54	80 100 120 150	220 240 280 320	E F G	J K L M	Q R S	V B E	VITRIFIED RESINOID SHELLAC
SILICON CARBIDE	C	16 20 24	60	180	400 500 600	H I	N O P	T U	R S	RUBBER SILICATE

STANDARD SYMBOLS FOR GRINDING WHEELS

SHARPENING TOOLS

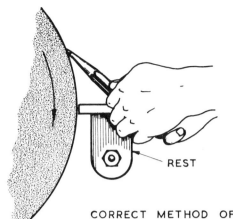

REST

CORRECT METHOD OF HOLDING
CHISELS, PUNCHES AND SCRIBERS
FOR OFF-HAND GRINDING

VERY LIGHT
PRESSURE ONLY

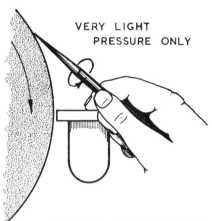

PUNCHES AND SCRIBERS
SHOULD BE ROTATED
WHILST GRINDING

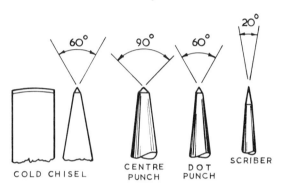

60° 90° 60° 20°

COLD CHISEL   CENTRE   DOT   SCRIBER   SCREWDRIVER
               PUNCH   PUNCH

LATHE TOOL BITS

8°

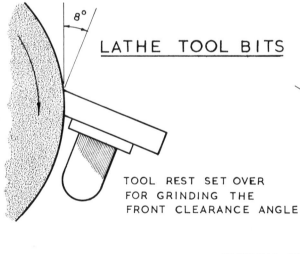

TOOL REST SET OVER
FOR GRINDING THE
FRONT CLEARANCE ANGLE

TWIST DRILLS

THE AXIS OF THE DRILL IS AT
59° TO THE WHEEL FACE AND
INCLINED UPWARDS FROM 8°
TO 10°.   THE CUTTING
EDGES ARE HORIZONTAL.
DOTTED LINES INDICATE
POSITION AT FINISH
OF SWEEP
ROUND

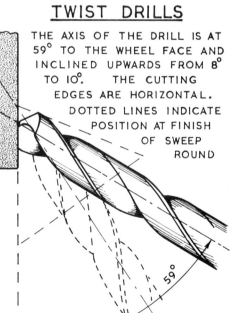

59°

GRINDING WHEEL

TOOLBIT

GRINDING SIDE AND
TOP RAKE ON THE
TOOL BIT

THE SHAPER

Shaping produces flat surfaces, including square-bottomed slots and vee-grooves, by traversing a reciprocating single point tool across the work. As the cutting action is similar to that of lathe tools, the range of tools used in the shaper is similar in profile and cutting angle to those used in the centre lathe, but the tools are usually heavier in section and are sometimes 'goose-necked' to reduce the tendency to dig in. The tool is held in a hinged tool post known as a 'clapper box'. This is free to pivot upwards lifting the cutting edge of the tool clear of the work on the return stroke. The weight of the tool post causes it to fall back into place as the ram reaches back-dead-centre bringing the cutting edge back into position for the next forward stroke. The tool post head, which carries a vertical feed and may also be swivelled, is secured to a ram which reciprocates along vee-shaped slides. The ram is driven by a crankpin mounted in a large driving wheel. The pin and its die block slide in a pivoted lever which, as shown in the diagram, gives a long slow cutting stroke at maximum power and a quick return stroke at minimum power. This slotted lever has either to be connected to the ram through a link arm in order to compensate for the variation in distance as the end of the slotted lever swings through an arc, or, as shown, the bottom end of the link arm is slotted to permit a compensating movement. A power feed may be applied to the table, which automatically advances the work whilst the tool is clear at the end of each return stroke.

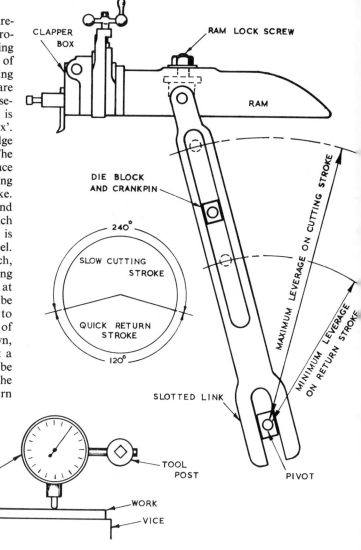

WORK CAN BE SET PARALLEL TO THE TRAVERSE WITH A DIAL GAUGE (DIAL INDICATOR)

TYPICAL SEQUENCE OF SHAPING OPERATIONS

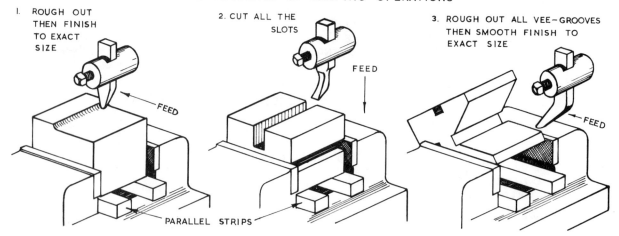

1. ROUGH OUT THEN FINISH TO EXACT SIZE

2. CUT ALL THE SLOTS

3. ROUGH OUT ALL VEE-GROOVES THEN SMOOTH FINISH TO EXACT SIZE

PARALLEL STRIPS

SAFETY IN THE WORKSHOP

HAZARDS

Accidents result most commonly for the following reasons:

Careless or hurried movement about the workshop causing collisions or knocking over of tools or materials. Careless movement is particularly dangerous near machinery.

Loose clothing or long hair becoming caught in revolving parts of machines, particularly the drilling and polishing machine spindles.

Failing to secure work properly before commencing machining.

Lack of care in handling hot metal.

GENERAL RULES FOR SAFETY

All injuries, no matter how slight, should be reported immediately.

Breakages and all damage to equipment should be reported.

A file should never be used without a handle.

The correct size and type of smith's tongs should be used when forging short work.

Hot work being transferred from forge to anvil should be held downwards close to the ground, to minimise danger of burns resulting from accidental collisions with other students.

When preparing the pickle bath for cleaning copper and gilding metal, the acid must be added to the water and never vice versa.

SAFETY RULES FOR MACHINE OPERATION

Before operating a machine secure all loose clothing, particularly cuffs, belts and ties.

Never clean moving machinery and never apply a rag or cotton waste to revolving work.

Swarf should always be removed with a brush and never with the fingers.

Always switch off a machine before clearing the swarf away from the job or the cutting tool.

Work being machined should never be held in the fingers but always secured in a chuck or vice, or bolted to the drill table, face plate or angle plate.

A machine should never be set in motion until all guards are securely in place.

After securing work in a lathe, shaping machine or milling machine, a check should be made to ensure that nothing will foul the moving parts and that the initial cut will be a light one.

Never leave a chuck key in a chuck.

If a machine appears to be faulty in operation it should be switched off and the matter reported immediately.

Goggles should always be worn when using a grinding wheel for tool sharpening.

One student only should operate the machine controls.

LIMITS AND FITS, POLISHING

LIMITS AND FITS

In order to produce interchangeable parts, essential for mass production, and to attain suitable fits on assembly, systems of limits and fits have been developed. The one generally used is the British Standard Institute System, this being similar to the International Standard System. Because holes are cut by standard-sized tools, drills and reamers, the size of the shaft is usually varied to suit the type of fit required.

The B S I system has three types of fit covering sixteen grades of accuracy. The fits are usually described as:

Clearance fit, which is a running fit.

Transition fit, which at the extremes may be either just easy or a light push fit.

Interference fit, where the shaft is always larger than the hole.

These fits are achieved by setting out the largest and smallest permissible dimensions about the nominal size for each type of fit. These dimensions are known as the 'high' and 'low' limits and the difference between them as the 'tolerance'. Reference tables are published giving the tolerances for all types of fits on all diameters.

POLISHING

Polishing consists of producing a smooth surface and is usually achieved by using abrasives of progressively decreasing grain size so that scratches on the metal surface are progressively reduced in size until they are so small as to be invisible to the naked eye.

With mild steel this is done by working down from second cut to smooth files, followed by draw-filing, preferably with chalk rubbed into the file teeth to prevent pinning, see page 29. Fine emery cloth is used next, either tightly wrapped round a file or glued to a flat piece of wood in order to preserve flat surfaces and square corners in the work. Oiled emery of FF grade drawn lengthways over the work will add the final polish.

Non-ferrous metals have initial blemishes ground out with water of ayr stone and then pickled in dilute acid to remove oxides. They are then planished on highly polished steel stakes and finally rubbed down on a power-driven buffing spindle. This carries mops loaded with fine abrasive composition. Good quality work is first polished on a linen mop and then after thorough washing is finished on a soft cotton mop dressed with rouge or crocus powder.

Polishing mops are made from 60 to 100 circular pieces of linen or cotton, sandwiched together between two strong leather washers.

Mops are spun at high speeds, loaded with a cutting compound made from sand, emery or rouge bonded in paraffin wax.

CLEARANCE FIT

SOURCES OF INFORMATION

BRITISH STANDARDS

The British Standards Institution, 2 Park Street, London W1Y 4AA, publish standards covering materials, tools and instruments used in most trades and professions. A full list of these is contained in the B S I yearbook. Details are given below of some standards which contain recommendations for metric dimensioning.

P D	5686	*The Use of S I Units*
B S	3763	*International System (S I) Units*
B S	3643	*I S O Metric Screw Threads*
B S	4318	*Recommendations for Basic Metric Sizes in Engineering*
B S	4500	*I S O Limits and Fits*
I S O	R 129	*Dimensioning Engineering Drawings*
B S	2045	*Preferred Numbers*
B S	192	*Supplement No 1. Open-ended Spanners*
B S	328	*Twist Drills*
B S	3692	*I S O Metric Screws, Bolts and Nuts*
B S	4183	*Metric Machine Screws and Nuts*
B S	4391	*Basic Metric Sizes for Metal Wire, Sheet and Strip*
P D	7308	*Engineering Drawing Practice for Schools and Colleges*

ASSOCIATIONS

The Associations listed below are always willing to assist with advice and information. They publish information leaflets and can usually supply the name and address of materials stockists.

Aluminium Federation, 60 Calthorpe Road, Edgbaston, Birmingham B15 1TM.
The British Oxygen Co. Ltd, Great West House, Brentford, Middlesex TW8 9AL.
Copper Development Association, Orchard House, Mutton Lane, Potters Bar, Herts.
British Steel Corporation, 9 Albert Embankment, London SE1 7SN.
Lead Development Association, 34 Berkeley Square, London W1X 6AJ
Tin Research Institute, Fraser Road, Perivale, Greenford, Middlesex.
Zinc Development Association, 34 Berkeley Square, London W1X 6AJ.

BRITISH STANDARD TWIST DRILL SIZES

Superseding drill gauge and letter sizes

Drill gauge and letter sizes of twist drills are now obsolete and should not be used in new designs. To assist users in securing the drill sizes required, the equivalent standard sizes are given below in bold type.

Old drill gauge and letter size		British Standard (international) series			Old drill gauge and letter size		British Standard (international) series			Old drill gauge and letter size		British Standard (international) series		
OLD SIZE	Decimal equivalent	NEW SIZE		Decimal equivalent	OLD SIZE	Decimal equivalent	NEW SIZE		Decimal equivalent	OLD SIZE	Decimal equivalent	NEW SIZE		Decimal equivalent
	in	mm	in	in		in	mm	in	in		in	mm	in	in
80	0.013 5	0.35		0.013 8	45	0.082 0	2.10		0.082 7	10	0.193 5	4.90		0.192 9
79	0.014 5	0.38		0.015 0	44	0.086 0	2.20		0.086 6	9	0.196 0	5.00		0.196 8
78	0.016 0	0.40		0.015 7	43	0.089 0	2.25		0.088 6	8	0.199 0	5.10		0.200 8
77	0.018 0	0.45		0.017 7	42	0.093 5		3/32	0.093 8	7	0.201 0	5.10		0.200 8
76	0.020 0	0.50		0.019 7	41	0.096 0	2.45		0.096 5	6	0.204 0	5.20		0.204 7
75	0.021 0	0.52		0.020 5	40	0.098 0	2.50		0.098 4	5	0.205 5	5.20		0.204 7
74	0.022 5	0.58		0.022 8	39	0.099 5	2.55		0.100 4	4	0.209 0	5.30		0.208 7
73	0.024 0	0.60		0.023 6	38	0.101 5	2.60		0.102 3	3	0.213 0	5.40		0.212 6
72	0.025 0	0.65		0.025 6	37	0.104 0	2.65		0.104 3	2	0.221 0	5.60		0.220 5
71	0.026 0	0.65		0.025 6	36	0.106 5	2.70		0.106 3	1	0.228 0	5.80		0.228 3
70	0.028 0	0.70		0.027 6	35	0.110 0	2.80		0.110 2	A	0.234 0		15/64	0.234 4
69	0.029 2	0.75		0.029 5	34	0.111 0	2.80		0.110 2	B	0.238 0	6.00		0.236 2
68	0.031 0		1/32	0.031 2	33	0.113 0	2.85		0.112 2	C	0.242 0	6.10		0.240 2
67	0.032 0	0.82		0.032 3	32	0.116 0	2.95		0.116 1	D	0.246 0	6.20		0.244 1
66	0.033 0	0.85		0.033 5	31	0.120 0	3.00		0.118 1	E	0.250 0		1/4	0.250 0
65	0.035 0	0.90		0.035 4	30	0.128 5	3.30		0.129 9	F	0.257 0	6.50		0.255 9
64	0.036 0	0.92		0.036 2	29	0.136 0	3.50		0.137 8	G	0.261 0	6.60		0.259 8
63	0.037 0	0.95		0.037 4	28	0.140 5		9/64	0.140 6	H	0.266 0		17/64	0.265 6
62	0.038 0	0.98		0.038 6	27	0.144 0	3.70		0.145 7	I	0.272 0	6.90		0.271 7
61	0.039 0	1.00		0.039 4	26	0.147 0	3.70		0.145 7	J	0.277 0	7.00		0.275 6
60	0.040 0	1.00		0.039 4	25	0.149 5	3.80		0.149 6	K	0.281 0		9/32	0.281 2
59	0.041 0	1.05		0.041 3	24	0.152 0	3.90		0.153 5	L	0.290 0	7.40		0.291 3
58	0.042 0	1.05		0.041 3	23	0.154 0	3.90		0.153 5	M	0.295 0	7.50		0.295 3
57	0.043 0	1.10		0.043 3	22	0.157 0	4.00		0.157 5	N	0.302 0	7.70		0.303 1
56	0.046 5		3/64	0.046 9	21	0.159 0	4.00		0.157 5	O	0.316 0	8.00		0.315 0
55	0.052 0	1.30		0.051 2	20	0.161 0	4.10		0.161 4	P	0.323 0	8.20		0.322 8
54	0.055 0	1.40		0.055 1	19	0.166 0	4.20		0.165 4	Q	0.332 0	8.40		0.330 7
53	0.059 5	1.50		0.059 1	18	0.169 5	4.30		0.169 3	R	0.339 0	8.60		0.338 6
52	0.063 5	1.60		0.063 0	17	0.173 0	4.40		0.173 2	S	0.348 0	8.80		0.346 5
51	0.067 0	1.70		0.066 9	16	0.177 0	4.50		0.177 2	T	0.358 0	9.10		0.358 3
50	0.070 0	1.80		0.070 9	15	0.180 0	4.60		0.181 1	U	0.368 0	9.30		0.366 1
49	0.073 0	1.85		0.072 8	14	0.182 0	4.60		0.181 1	V	0.377 0		3/8	0.375 0
48	0.076 0	1.95		0.076 8	13	0.185 0	4.70		0.185 0	W	0.386 0	9.80		0.385 8
47	0.078 5	2.00		0.078 7	12	0.189 0	4.80		0.189 0	X	0.397 0	10.10		0.397 6
46	0.081 0	2.05		0.080 7	11	0.191 0	4.90		0.192 9	Y	0.404 0	10.30		0.405 5
										Z	0.413 0	10.50		0.413 4

B S.328 A 1963: *Twist drill sizes, superseding drill gauge and letter sizes* is reproduced by permission of the British Standards Institution, 2 Park Street, London W1Y 4AA, from whom copies of the data sheet may be obtained.

REFERENCE DATA

ISO METRIC SCREW THREADS All dimensions are in millimetres					
OUTSIDE DIAMETER *Preferred Sizes*	PITCH *Coarse Series*	TAPPING DRILL *Coarse Series*	PITCH *Fine Series*	TAPPING DRILL *Fine Series*	CLEARANCE DRILL *Medium Fit*
1.6	0.35	1.30	0.2	1.32	1.8
2	0.4	1.60	0.25	1.68	2.25
2.5	0.45	2.05	0.35	2.15	2.8
3	0.5	2.50	0.35	2.62	3.4
4	0.7	3.40	0.5	3.50	4.5
5	0.8	4.30	0.5	4.40	5.5
6	1.0	5.10	0.75	5.20	6.6
8	1.25	6.90	1.0	7.0	9.0
10	1.5	8.60	1.25	9.0	11.0
12	1.75	10.40	1.25	11.0	14.0
16	2.0	14.00	1.50	15.0	18.0
20	2.5	17.50	1.50	19.0	22.0

NOTE: All drill sizes given are slightly larger than standard recommendations and holes drilled to these sizes will produce a thread having about 65 per cent of the nominal depth. This is sufficient for general use and it will be found that the slightly oversize hole lessens the risk of tap breakage.

According to published tables, fine pitch screws larger than M5 may have two, three or four different pitch sizes. The sizes quoted above are in agreement with the first choice recommendations in BS 3643.

APPROXIMATE R.P.M. FOR H.S. DRILLS			
Drill Size	Mild Steel	Brass	Aluminium
3 mm	3000	5000	6000
4.5 mm	2000	3500	4500
6 mm	1600	2500	3500
8 mm	1300	2000	3000
10 mm	1000	1800	2500
11 mm	900	1600	2000
12 mm	700	1300	1500

FLUXES FOR SOLDERING	
Steel	Zinc Chloride
Tinplate	Zinc Chloride or Resin
Copper, Brass	Zinc Chloride or Resin
Zinc	Dilute Hydrochloric Acid
Lead	Tallow

CUTTING FLUIDS USED IN TAPPING AND THREADING			
Aluminium	Mild Steel	Brass	Cast Iron
Paraffin	Lard Oil Soluble Oil	Paraffin	Dry

REFERENCE DATA

BRITISH STANDARD WHITWORTH SCREW THREADS			
Screw Diameter	Tapping Drill	Clearing Drill	T.P.I.
$\frac{1}{8}''$	No. 40	$\frac{9}{64}''$	40
$\frac{3}{16}''$	No. 27	$\frac{13}{64}''$	24
$\frac{1}{4}''$	No. 10	$\frac{17}{64}''$	20
$\frac{5}{16}''$	Letter F	$\frac{21}{64}''$	18
$\frac{3}{8}''$	Letter N	$\frac{25}{64}''$	16
$\frac{7}{16}''$	$\frac{23}{64}''$	$\frac{29}{64}''$	14
$\frac{1}{2}''$	$\frac{13}{32}''$	$\frac{33}{64}''$	12

BRITISH STANDARD FINE SCREW THREADS			
Screw Diameter	Tapping Drill	Clearing Drill	T.P.I.
$\frac{1}{4}''$	$\frac{7}{32}''$	Letter F	26
$\frac{5}{16}''$	$\frac{17}{64}''$	Letter P	22
$\frac{3}{8}''$	$\frac{21}{64}''$	Letter W	20
$\frac{7}{16}''$	$\frac{3}{8}''$	$\frac{29}{64}''$	18
$\frac{1}{2}''$	$\frac{27}{64}''$	$\frac{33}{64}''$	16
$\frac{9}{16}''$	$\frac{31}{64}''$	$\frac{37}{64}''$	16
$\frac{5}{8}''$	$\frac{35}{64}''$	$\frac{41}{64}''$	14

B.A. SCREW THREADS		
Screw Size	Tapping Drill	Clearing Drill
No. 8	No. 50	$\frac{3}{32}''$
No. 7	No. 46	$\frac{7}{64}''$
No. 6	No. 43	$\frac{1}{8}''$
No. 5	No. 37	$\frac{9}{64}''$
No. 4	No. 32	$\frac{5}{32}''$
No. 3	No. 28	$\frac{11}{64}''$
No. 2	No. 24	$\frac{3}{16}''$
No. 1	No. 17	$\frac{7}{32}''$
No. 0	No. 10	$\frac{1}{4}''$

Details of obsolete threads and drills are included to help with using up old stock.

COMMON ABBREVIATIONS

A/F	Across flats
CRS	Centres
CI	Cast iron
CL or ₵	Centre line
CH HD	Cheese head
CS	Carbon steel
CSK	Countersunk
CSK HD	Countersunk head
C'BORE	Counterbore
DIA	Diameter*
Ø	Diameter†
HEX	Hexagon
HEX HD	Hexagon head
HSS	High speed steel
MS	Mild steel
PCD	Pitch circle diameter
RAD	Radius*
R	Radius†
RD HD	Round head
SCR	Screwed
S'FACE	Spotface
SQ	Square*
□	Square†
U'CUT	Undercut
WI	Wrought iron

* when used in note form
† when set before a drawing dimension

REFERENCE DATA

Millimetres to inches

Milli-metres	0	1	2	3	4	5	6	7	8	9
					INCHES					
0	—	0·039	0·079	0·118	0·157	0·197	0·236	0·276	0·315	0·354
10	0·394	0·433	0·472	0·512	0·551	0·591	0·630	0·669	0·709	0·748
20	0·787	0·827	0·866	0·906	0·945	0·984	1·024	1·063	1·102	1·142
30	1·181	1·220	1·260	1·299	1·339	1·378	1·417	1·457	1·496	1·535
40	1·575	1·614	1·654	1·693	1·732	1·772	1·811	1·850	1·890	1·929
50	1·969	2·008	2·047	2·087	2·126	2·165	2·205	2·244	2·284	2·323
60	2·362	2·402	2·441	2·480	2·520	2·559	2·598	2·638	2·677	2·717
70	2·756	2·795	2·835	2·874	2·913	2·953	2·992	3·032	3·071	3·110
80	3·150	3·190	3·228	3·268	3·307	3·347	3·386	3·425	3·465	3·504
90	3·543	3·583	3·622	3·661	3·701	3·740	3·780	3·819	3·858	3·898
100	3·937	3·976	4·016	4·055	4·095	4·134	4·173	4·213	4·252	4·291
110	4·331	4·370	4·410	4·449	4·488	4·528	4·567	4·606	4·646	4·685
120	4·724	4·764	4·803	4·843	4·882	4·921	4·961	5·000	5·039	5·079
130	5·118	5·158	5·197	5·236	5·276	5·315	5·354	5·394	5·433	5·473
140	5·512	5·551	5·591	5·630	5·669	5·709	5·748	5·788	5·827	5·866
150	5·906	5·945	5·984	6·024	6·063	6·102	6·142	6·181	6·221	6·260
160	6·299	6·339	6·378	6·417	6·457	6·496	6·536	6·575	6·614	6·654
170	6·693	6·732	6·772	6·811	6·851	6·890	6·929	6·969	7·008	7·047
180	7·087	7·126	7·165	7·205	7·244	7·284	7·323	7·362	7·402	7·441
190	7·480	7·520	7·559	7·599	7·638	7·677	7·717	7·756	7·795	7·835
200	7·874	7·914	7·953	7·992	8·032	8·071	8·110	8·150	8·189	8·228
210	8·268	8·307	8·347	8·386	8·425	8·465	8·504	8·543	8·583	8·622
220	8·662	8·701	8·740	8·780	8·819	8·858	8·898	8·937	8·977	9·016
230	9·055	9·095	9·134	9·173	9·213	9·252	9·292	9·331	9·370	9·410
240	9·449	9·488	9·528	9·567	9·606	9·646	9·685	9·725	9·764	9·803
250	9·843	9·882	9·921	9·961	10·00	10·04	10·08	10·12	10·16	10·20
260	10·24	10·28	10·31	10·35	10·39	10·43	10·47	10·51	10·55	10·59
270	10·63	10·67	10·71	10·75	10·79	10·83	10·87	10·91	10·95	10·98
280	11·02	11·06	11·10	11·14	11·18	11·22	11·26	11·30	11·34	11·38
290	11·42	11·46	11·50	11·54	11·58	11·61	11·65	11·69	11·73	11·77
300	11·81	11·85	11·89	11·93	11·97	12·01	12·05	12·09	12·13	12·17
310	12·20	12·24	12·28	12·32	12·36	12·40	12·44	12·48	12·52	12·56
320	12·60	12·64	12·68	12·72	12·76	12·80	12·83	12·87	12·91	12·95
330	12·99	13·03	13·07	13·11	13·15	13·19	13·23	13·27	13·31	13·35
340	13·39	13·43	13·46	13·50	13·54	13·58	13·62	13·66	13·70	13·74
350	13·78	13··82	13·86	13·90	13·94	13·98	14·02	14·06	14·09	14·13
360	14·17	14·21	14·25	14·29	14·33	14·37	14·41	14·45	14·49	14·53
370	14·57	14·61	14·65	14·69	14·72	14·76	14·80	14·84	14·88	14·92
380	14·96	15·00	15·04	15·08	15·12	15·16	15·20	15·24	15·28	15·32
390	15·35	15·39	15·43	15·47	15·51	15·55	15·59	15 63	15·67	15·71
400	15·75	15·79	15·83	15·87	15·91	15·95	15·98	16·02	16·06	16·10
410	16·14	16·18	16·22	16·26	16·30	16·34	16·38	16·42	16·46	16·50
420	16·54	16·58	16·61	16·65	16·69	16·73	16·77	16·81	16·85	16·89
430	16·93	16·97	17·01	17·05	17·09	17·13	17·17	17·21	17·24	17·28
440	17·32	17·36	17·40	17·44	17·48	17·52	17·56	17·60	17·64	17·68
450	17·72	17·76	17·80	17·83	17·87	17·91	17·95	17·99	18·03	18·07
460	18·11	18·15	18·19	18·23	18·27	18·31	18·35	18·39	18·43	18·46
470	18·50	18·54	18·58	18·62	18·66	18·70	18·74	18·78	18·82	18·86
480	18·90	18·94	18·98	19·02	19·06	19·09	19·13	19·17	19·21	19·25
490	19·29	19·33	19·37	19·41	19·45	19·49	19·53	19·57	19·61	19·65

Reproduced by courtesy of J. Smith and Sons Ltd of Clerkenwell.

METRICATION IN METALWORK

It was decided in 1965 that British industry would adopt the metric system. The Government, in giving support to this move, expressed the hope that by 1975 the greater part of industry would have made the change.

In going metric Britain is adopting the International System of Units, abbreviated to the initials 'S I' throughout the world. S I is based on and incorporates the metric system. An important feature of S I is that units for all purposes can be derived in a rational and coherent way and it is therefore suitable for all applications. The S I system was proposed by the General Conference on Weights and Measures in 1960 and is being adopted by almost all countries of the world.

Metrication is not just a matter of changing the system of measurement, but involves considerable modification to existing standards and practices. For instance, in Britain we have a preferred range of sizes based on fractions of an inch such as $\frac{1}{8}$, $\frac{1}{4}$, $\frac{3}{8}$, $\frac{1}{2}$ and so on, and this has led to the production of standard material sizes expressed in these terms. It would be uneconomical to convert these fractional inch sizes to metric equivalents, therefore industry is adopting a new series of preferred sizes. These sizes are listed in British Standard 4318,

Recommendations for Preferred Metric Basic Sizes for Engineering. This range is based on a geometric progression in which each successive number represents a constant percentage increase over the previous number. This is preferable to the arithmetic series in which 1 to 2 represents a 100% increase but 9 to 10 represents only about a 10% increase. British Standard Specifications often give three columns of sizes representing a first, second and third choice series: the aim being to encourage maximum use of a limited number of sizes given in the first choice series thus restricting the variety of stock sizes to a minimum.

It has been found, however, that stock holders, whilst following the BSI recommendation in stocking the first choice range of preferred metric sizes, are also stocking a number of sizes in the second choice range. This will be helpful during the change-over period in that existing imperial designs can be continued for a while with a minimum of modification.

When selecting material sizes, tools and other dimensions, to gain maximum benefit from this change to the metric system, the first choice preferred sizes should be used whenever possible.

PREFERRED SIZES, IN MILLIMETRES, FOR METALWORK				
1	16	75	190	600
1.2	20	80	200	650
1.6	25	90	220	700
2	30	100	240	750
2.5	35	110	260	800
3	40	120	280	900
4	45	130	300	1000
5	50	140	350	1200
6	55	150	400	1500
8	60	160	450	2000
10	65	170	500	2500
12	70	180	550	3000

(BS 4318)

QUESTIONS

The key to the abbreviations of the Examining Boards is given on page 2.

Materials

1. (a) Describe the properties of (i) copper and (ii) cast iron and state two examples of the use of each.
   (b) What is an alloy? Name three alloys commonly found in the workshop and state one use and the composition of each. (UL)
2. Describe briefly the processes involved in manufacturing mild steel bar from iron ore. (UL)
3. If you were given four unidentified pieces of ferrous metal known to be cast iron, wrought iron, cast steel and mild steel respectively, what tests would you apply to identify them? Illustrate from the workshop a use for each metal and state what qualities make it suitable for its particular purpose. (OLE)
4. What are the main differences between the metals used for (a) binding wire, as used during hard soldering, (b) vice jaws, (c) bases of scribing blocks? Name the particular kind of metal used for each and describe briefly how one of the metals is manufactured. (OLE)
5. (a) Sketch a 'Bessemer Converter', naming its main parts, and describe, briefly, the method of manufacturing steel by this process.
   (b) Name an alternative process used for steel manufacture, giving the basic differences between the two processes. (AEB)
6. Carbon steels are often divided into three main groups according to carbon-content range and the associated properties. Name these groups, giving the approximate carbon-content range and describe briefly the properties of the steels in each range. (AEB)
7. (a) Make a sketch of the iron-carbon diagram for plain carbon steels up to 1.4% carbon, indicating the important parts of the diagram, including the hardening and annealing zones.
   (b) Define the terms 'annealing' and 'normalising' as applied to plain carbon steels. (AEB)
8. Describe the cementation method of producing steel. Why did Huntsman's process give a better steel? (JMB)
9. Discuss the contribution to the steel industry of Sidney Thomas and Percy Gilchrist. (JMB)
10. Give descriptions in note form of workshop tests to distinguish between carbon steel and mild steel. What is the difference between hardening and case-hardening? (SUJB)
11. Name four different ferrous metals or alloys and write brief notes on each describing their characteristics and working properties. (SUJB)
12. What is the main use of the open hearth furnace? With the aid of a sectional diagram, explain the process.
   What particular function is performed by the 'chequer' chambers? (WJEC)
13. What is the difference between a ferrous metal and a non-ferrous metal? (EAEB)
14. Name two non-ferrous alloys and the substances from which they are made. (SREB)
15. What methods are adopted in the workshop to identify the common varieties of iron and steel? Tabulate your answer.
16. Compare and contrast the properties of the following metals: (a) mild steel, cast steel, (b) copper, brass.
17. What is galvanised iron? State some of its uses.

Measuring and Marking Out

18. Give the name of a tool specifically designed for accurate testing of (a) horizontal levels, (b) narrow gaps, (c) depth of blind holes, (d) angles, (e) internal diameters, (f) spherical roundness, (g) internal and external radii.
   Sketch two of the tools you have mentioned and briefly describe their particular features and the method of using them. (OLE)
19. (a) Describe a method of measuring accurately:
   (i) the length and diameter of a blind hole, 25 mm diameter and 25 mm deep.
   (ii) the diameter, length and straightness of a shaft 25 mm diameter, 150 mm long.
   (b) Make a neat, annotated sketch of a 'go' and 'not go' plug gauge.
20. (a) State the principle upon which the micrometer is based. Sketch a type of internal micrometer.
   (b) Explain how you would drill a number of blind holes of equal depth. (AEB)
21. How would a piece of round bar be held when marking out with a surface gauge? (EAEB)
22. Name two tools you would use in conjunction with a surface plate. (ALSEB)
23. Describe, with sketches, how you would mark off the centre of a 25 mm dia. bar.
24. Describe two methods of marking a line parallel to a straight edge.
25. Name six marking out tools, sketch two of these and describe their use.
26. What is understood by a Vernier Scale?
27. Sketch a micrometer thimble and sleeve showing them set at a reading of 11.75 mm.

Hand Tools

28. Sketch and name the hand tools normally used in the workshop to cut both internal and external threads. When forming mating pieces which thread would you cut first and why? Describe the method of cutting an external thread. (OLE)
29. Make a neat freehand sketch of a hacksaw and show in an enlarged drawing how the tension is put on the blade. When replacing a blade what precautions do you take? Give reasons why hacksaw blades can be purchased having 18, 24, and 32 T. (OLE)
30. (a) Make a large sketch of a handled half round file naming the parts.
   (b) What is (i) drawfiling, (ii) pinning?
   (c) Sketch two forms of vice clamps.
   (d) Is a file uniformly tempered throughout? Give reasons for your answer. (OLE)
31. Sketch and describe the uses of the following hand tools:
   (a) a flat scraper,
   (b) a 'rat-tail' file,
   (c) a crosscut chisel. (AEB)
32. A die-holder for circular dies has three adjusting screws. Make drawings of these screws and show by further drawings how their adjustment affects the function of the die.
   Explain the effect of die adjustment in relation to:
   (a) The process of thread cutting.
   (b) Accuracy of the thread being cut.
   (c) The fit of the nut. (SUJB)

33. Discuss the use of hacksaw blades in relation to the metal to be sawn.

Explain the terms 'kerf' and 'set' in relation to hacksawing. How is the set produced on (a) coarse tooth blades and (b) fine tooth blades?

34. Explain, with the aid of drawings, the essential similarities, and differences, between metric coarse and metric fine screw threads. Say what are the special advantages of each.

Given two taps similar in design and quality, one metric coarse and the other metric fine, say which is the more fragile and why?

35. (a) Make sectional profile sketches of any *two* of the following screw threads, indicating, in each case, the angle and a suitable use to which the threads are put:

(i) British Standard Whitworth.
(ii) Acme,
(iii) Buttress.

(b) Explain in detail how you would drill and tap an M 10 thread into a piece of 12 mm thick mild steel plate.

36. Describe, with the aid of sketches, how a hacksaw blade is held taut and straight in the frame. How many teeth would a blade have to cut 10 mm thick mild steel.

37. (a) Name *four* vices used in the metal workshop, and make a clear sketch of *one* of them.

(b) State the thread form of the main screw of each of the four vices named, giving reasons for the use of the particular thread in each case. (*CLE*)

Joining Metals

38. Describe with sketches how you would join to-gether two pieces of heavy gauge sheet metal using rivets to show:

(a) the rivets finishing flush with the surfaces,
(b) round snap heads of the rivets showing on each face. (*UL*)

39. Sketch the bit and part of the shank of both a straight and hatchet pattern soldering iron, naming and giving reasons for the materials used in their manufacture.

Describe two different methods of joining metal with solder. (*OLE*)

40. Name suitable fluxes which may be used when soldering:

(a) wires in an electrical circuit,
(b) two pieces of sheet tin plate,
(c) two pieces of brass (hard soldered).

Give your reasons why the fluxes you have named are suitable.

Describe *one* of the processes used in (a), (b) *or* (c). (*UL*)

41. Assume that you are required to make an open topped tinplate box 120 x 80 x 25 mm high, the sides of which are all perpendicular to the base and wired on the top edge.

(a) Draw a development of the box, showing all joint and wiring allowances.

(b) Draw a series of sketches to illustrate the methods and tools used when bending *all four sides*. (*OLE*)

42. Make neat sketches of *three* joints commonly used in sheetmetalwork practice and comment on the most suitable application of each type of joint. Sketch and describe briefly the method of producing one of the joints selected. (*AEB*)

43. (a) Describe the possible uses of (i) welded joints, (ii) soldered joints, and (iii) riveted joints, and compare their advantages and disadvantages.

(b) Sketch three types of rivet heads. (*AEB*)

44. Analyse the following faults that can occur when brazing mild steel and suggest suitable remedies.

When heating a piece of round stock in a blind hole the rod jumps out of the hole.

Spelter forms into balls and fails to run into the joint.

Molten spelter fails to run the full length of a well-prepared butt joint 50 mm long in mild steel 3 mm thick.

45. Describe, step by step, how you would soft-solder the following:

The corner of a tinplate box. An electrical connection on a radio. (*ALSEB*)

46. Explain how you would make the following in Tin Plate.

(a) A folded and grooved seam.
(b) A wired edge.

Sketch one example of a job in which each might be used. (*SEREB*)

47. Give *two* reasons why a flux is necessary when soft soldering. (*EAEB*)

48. Describe in detail how you would prepare and make ready for use a new soldering bit (iron). Sketch:

(i) an ordinary straight soldering bit,
(ii) a hatchet soldering bit.

State which solders and fluxes are commonly used with these tools. (*SREB*)

49. What riveting allowance would be used to form a snap head?

Forgework. Heat Treatment

50. Make a sectional diagram through a water-cooled forge tuyère showing the position of the fire relative to it. What precautions would you take to prevent a dirty forge fire? Sketch a 'C' scroll and an 'S' scroll and a tool which you would use to form them. (*OLE*)

51. What do you understand by the tempering of steel and why is it necessary? What are the colours and approximate temperatures to which the following tools should be tempered: (a) screwdriver, (b) cold chisel, (c) centre punch, (d) scriber? (*OLE*)

52. Steels are sometimes described as high carbon, medium carbon, or low carbon. Say what is meant by these terms, particularly with regard to the processes of hardening and tempering.

What difficulties would you expect to encounter when hammering over a mild steel rivet, and how would you overcome them? (*SUJB*)

53. Write brief notes on the process of case hardening, concluding with notes on the advantages and disadvantages of the method.

Comment on the kind of steel articles suitable for case hardening and those that are not. Give two or three actual examples. (*SUJB*)

54. Describe, with a sketch, how you would forge, harden and temper a cross-cut chisel to cut 4 mm grooves in mild steel. Sketch the angle of the cutting edge. (*AEB*)

55. State how you would harden:

(a) a piece of tool steel,
(b) a piece of mild steel,

What is the essential difference between (a) and (b) after hardening? (*AEB*)

56. What is meant by 'upper and lower critical points' when referring to the heat treatment of plain carbon steel? What effect does variation in carbon content of plain carbon steel have on its behaviour when heated? Illustrate with sketches. (*AEB*)

57. Make carefully-drawn sketches of the following forge tools:

(*a*) a swage,

(*b*) a fuller,

(*c*) a flatter.

With illustrations, describe a suitable use for each of these tools. (*WMEB*)

58. Show, by means of a sketch, what is meant by up-setting. (*EAEB*)

59. Make a large freehand sketch of a blacksmith's anvil. Name the parts and indicate the use of each part. (*EAEB*)

60. Why is it necessary to temper a tool after it has been hardened? (*MREB*)

61. (*a*) Explain the difference between hardening and tempering and case hardening.

(*b*) Give one example of a tool that you have made or used where it has been:

(*i*) hardened and tempered,

(*ii*) case hardened. (*SEREB*)

62. By what process could the surface of a small piece of mild steel be made harder? (*EAEB*)

Beaten Metalwork

63. A depression or a 'well' 100 mm dia. and 20 mm deep is to be made in the centre of a 150 mm dia. piece of sheet copper. With the assistance of a series of diagrams describe how you would make the 'well'.

64. Give *three* reasons for planishing a piece of hammered metalwork. (*EAEB*)

65. Make a sketch to show how you would wire up a small copper cylinder, e.g. a serviette ring, prior to silver soldering the joint. (*SREB*)

66. What is the name of the process which softens brass, copper and gilding metal?

How could you re-harden these metals? (*ALSEB*)

67. Sketch any three of the following hammer heads and explain their uses: raising hammer, planishing hammer, paning hammer, collet hammer, doming hammer.

68. Name two important tools used when hollowing a copper dish.

69. What solution is contained in the acid bath which helps clean annealed copper and gilding metal?

70. Describe briefly the main difference between hollowing and raising.

Casting

71. Show by reference to a practical example, from your own experience if possible, how a sand mould is prepared up to the stage of pouring the metal, using a one-piece pattern. (*CLE*)

72. Explain what is meant by each of the following terms, as applied to the production of castings:

(*a*) pouring gate and feeding gate,

(*b*) runner,

(*c*) core print.

Why is it sometimes necessary to use split patterns? (*AEB*)

73. List the main stages of casting in sand, a name plate or plant label in aluminium. Use sketches to illustrate your answer. (*SEREB*)

74. Explain the need for 'draft' on patterns used in casting. (*SREB*)

75. Make simple sketches of *three* tools or pieces of equipment that are used in foundrywork. Explain briefly how each one is used. (*SEREB*)

76. Draw a labelled section through a sand mould which is ready for casting.

77. What is a 'blowhole' in a casting?

78. How is parting sand used and what is its function?

79. What is meant by 'cope' and 'drag'?

80. What are the vent holes in a sand mould?

Workshop Machines

81. Name the tools used to make the following holes and sketch and describe the important features of their cutting parts:

(*a*) a 5 mm diameter hole in mild steel,

(*b*) holes drilled in the ends of a mild steel bar in preparation for centre turning.

(*c*) a 40 mm diameter hole in sheet metal.

82. Use sketches and notes to illustrate:

(*a*) the mechanism for raising and lowering the spindle of a sensitive drilling machine.

(*b*) the provision made in the spindle for removing the drill chuck and the method of its removal. (*CLE*)

83. Most drilling machines can operate at different speeds. How is this done and why is it essential? (*OLE*)

84. (*a*) In what circumstances would you use a reamer?

(*b*) Why does a twist drill sometimes become 'blued' when in use?

(*c*) State the coolants (if any) you would use when machining (*i*) mild steel, (*ii*) brass, (*iii*) bronze, (*iv*) aluminium, (*v*) cast iron.

(*d*) Describe the operations in cutting an M 12 thread on the end of a rod.

85. Why must a centre punch be used before drilling? (*EAEB*)

86. Taper turning can be effected by off-setting the tail stock of a lathe. By simple diagrams show exactly what you would do to turn a taper of 1 in 14 on a 100 x 25 mm dia. piece of mild steel so that the smaller end would be at the tail stock end. What tests would you carry out to ensure that the tail stock had been replaced correctly for parallel turning?

87. (*a*) Describe how you would drill an 8 mm dia. hole 20 mm deep along the central axis of a 50 mm dia. mild steel bar 50 mm long, using a lathe. Assume that the ends of the bar have already been faced to length.

(*b*) Describe how you would enlarge the hole to a diameter of 20 mm by 25 mm deep. Sketch the working end of the tool used.

88. Show by means of sketches and brief descriptions how:

(*a*) the tailstock is held to the bed of a lathe,

(*b*) the centre is held in the spindle of the tailstock,

(*c*) the spindle is moved in the tailstock, as when bringing the centre up to the work,

(*d*) the spindle is locked in position in the tailstock. (*UL*)

89. Sketch *three* views of a parting tool and indicate the top rake and front and side clearance angles. What precautions must be taken in setting up the tool in the lathe tool post? (*JMB*)

90. Describe, with the aid of a diagrammatic sketch, how the back gear of a lathe works, and explain the reason for its use. (*WJEC*)

91. Describe briefly, with sketches where helpful, the meaning of *five* of the following lathework terms: centre, cross slide, tolerance, radiusing, surfacing, rake, parting, feed. (*SUJB*)

92. (*a*) What factors should be taken into consideration in selecting suitable cutting speeds and feeds when operating a centre lathe?

(*b*) What effects will excessive overhang of job and of tool have on a turning operation?

(*c*) Sketch a parting-off tool and describe the precaution that must be taken in its use. (*AEB*)

93. Discuss the relative merits and limitations of 3-jaw and 4-jaw chucks, paying particular attention to:

(*a*) the accuracy of final set up,

(*b*) the time taken to achieve satisfactory setting.
(*AEB*)

94. A piece of work to be machined in the lathe may be held:

(*a*) between centres,

(*b*) in a 3-jaw self-centring chuck,

(*c*) in a 4-jaw independent chuck,

Give *one* example of the correct use of each method.
(*AEB*)

95. For certain work, e.g., drilling a 7 mm dia. hole on the longitudinal axis of a 50 mm piece of 20 mm dia. mild steel, it is more accurate to use a lathe rather than a drilling machine and machine vice. Account for this, sketch the lathe set up to do the work and describe how the work is done. (*OLE*)

96. Make a simple line drawing to show how you would set up a lathe to turn a round bar between centres.

Name the main parts shown in your drawing.
(*SEREB*)

97. Compare the action of emery cloth on metal with that of a grinding machine. What is the approximate spindle speed of a grinding machine? What is the nature of the composition of grinding wheels that they can wear away steel yet in time they themselves become worn away? (*SUJB*)

98. (*a*) What precautions should be taken when using an off-hand grinding machine? What precautions should be taken when fitting a new wheel to ensure, as far as possible, the safety of the operator?

(*b*) What instructions should be given to operators to ensure a reasonable wheel life? (*AEB*)

99. What is the general rule for choosing drilling speeds for different sized holes?

100. Sketch a centre drill and explain its use.

Safety

101. What safety precautions must be observed in school metal workshops when using the following?

(*a*) a drilling machine,

(*b*) a spindle polisher,

(*c*) an acid pickle.

In each case, emphasise any dangers and the ways in which these can be avoided. (*CLE*)

102. The hammered ends of cold chisels and forging tools often become badly burred. Why are they dangerous to use in this state, and what can be done to restore them to a safe condition? (*CLE*)

103. Electrical power is used extensively in the modern workshop. What precautions should be taken to prevent accidents when using electrically operated equipment? State briefly what immediate action should be taken when a person suffers from electric shock? (*AEB*)

104. State *two* safety precautions which must be taken when using a power drilling machine. (*EAEB*)

105. State the most important safety precaution that should be taken when drilling sheet metal with a drilling machine. (*MEB*)

106. What dangers are there in the following circumstances?

(*a*) Wearing loose clothing when using a machine tool

(*b*) Lifting heavy objects

(*c*) Using a buffing machine

(*d*) Using a cold chisel. (*ALSEB*)

107. Comment on the need for: (*a*) good lighting, (*b*) good heating, (*c*) good ventilation, in relation to the prevention of accidents in the workshops. (*AEB*)

108. What general precautions should be taken when using acids in the workshop?

109. Why is it especially dangerous to clean moving machinery?

110. Why should machinery guards never be removed without official permission?

CONVERSION SCALE

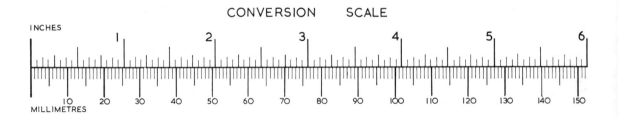

INDEX